HELICOPTER ESSENTIALS

AIRCREW SURVIVAL MANUAL

HEMS HELICOPTER ESSENTIALS
AIRCREW SURVIVAL MANUAL

By

Chris 'Razor' Sharpe

With forwards by

'Jungle Jimmy' McSparron, Fellow of the Explorers Club

And

'Wolf 2', Chief Warrant Officer (CW3), United States Army

This document is intended solely as a guide to the appropriate standards and procedures employed by crewmembers whilst rendering engaged in helicopter operations including pre, post-crash and emergency situations. It is not intended as a statement of the standards required in any situation, because circumstances and conditions can vary widely from one country to another. Nor is it intended that this document shall in anyway advise personnel concerning legal authority to perform the procedures discussed.

The procedures and protocols in this document are based on the most current recommendations of responsible sources. Other or additional safety measures may be required under circumstances present at the material time.

Copyright © 2019 by Black Wolf Helicopter Special Operations Aviation & Training / BW Consultancy

All rights reserved

ISBN: 9781713045441

Dedicated to my wonderful partner, Telma Canel, who has had to live with both me and helicopters, my son Eddie who has suffered living without me due to helicopters and whom without this book would not have been possible.

FORWARD

After a decade in terrestrial search and rescue as well as a lifetime learning and practicing the intricacies of survival in remote environments, I finally took the plunge into the world of para medicine in my early thirties.

During my wanderings I've met many characters, few of whom have had such an impact as Chris "Razor" Sharpe. Every now and then one has the privilege to come across an individual that makes an impact, not only on your own life but those around you. I knew from the moment we met that we were destined to collaborate on many missions and projects around the world and that is exactly what has happened.

Chris' experience, in flight medicine and helicopter search and rescue, runs into tens of thousands of hours with the number of successful rescues soaring into unimaginable numbers. However, despite all this, he is still one of the humblest men I've ever met. A relaxed but clearly wise demeanor firmly grips every conversation and his ability to educate you without even trying never ceases to amaze me.

We work in an industry that has safety at its heart and this book contains information gained over three decades of service, both military and civilian. It contains insight you won´t find in normal courses. It encompasses everything you need to make yourself a better, more experienced and safer member of the team. It is the definitive guide to everything aircrew survival related and something you will want to keep close to you at all times. Every helicopter company should have one of these in their survival kits.

Currently working alongside Air Andes Helicopters, Jimmy has spent his life in some of the most remote jungles on the planet. He has featured both on and off screen with National Geographic, the BBC and Channel 4 and is a well-known Jungle Survival Instructor.

Recently confirmed as a member of The Faculty of Conflict and Catastrophe Medicine – Worshipful Society of Apothecaries and awarded fellowships at the Royal Geographic Society, Royal Anthropological Institute and even the noted Explorers Club as well as being an Ambassador for the Craghoppers clothing range. Outside of the jungle, Jimmy has ridden a horse 600 miles across the second highest plain in the world, driven a 3 wheeled tuk-tuk 2500 miles across the whole of Peru and been part of earthquake relief teams in Indonesia.

Four years ago, I first met Chris 'Razor' Sharpe briefly at an airshow in Central America, where his helicopter crew had been conducting a rescue display. I was impressed with his professionalism, knowledge, experience and his drive and passion to increase helicopter rear crew safety and operational standards to support us as the Pilots in our mission framework.

Since we met, Razor was awarded the 2019 Helicopter Association International 'Salute to Excellence' Safety Award for his promotion of safety within the International helicopter community. From being the Project Manager for the HeliSOS Helicopter Rescue/Air Ambulance service to teaching local military special forces aircrews and despite language barriers continually pushing organizations to change and improve their training. As his award stated, much of this has been done in his own time with his own money in order to show people, that safe helicopter operations do not require extensive budgets. Just a sensible approach to keeping all of us in the airframe – alive.

In this book, Razor takes the reader from the crew room and the essential briefings, risk mitigation strategies, to the 'Dress to Egress', and an introduction to the many different types of flight clothing and survival equipment available for differing climates. As a Survival manual, it focuses on preventing the emergency in the first place, but if we do crash or ditch in water, the equipment and survival skills that we need to live.

When I first read the draft manuscript, my only comment was, 'this is what we do every day in the military' but written by a Chief Aircrewman with over 15,000 hours flight time in a style that is a pleasure to read.

He has provided an Aircrew Survival manual truly different to all the others, based on experiences, both good and bad and has provided all of us involved in helicopter operations a manual that all of us in this profession will benefit from.

For this, we are truly grateful.

Wolf 2 is an active duty Chief Warrant Officer (CW3) Helicopter Instructor Pilot with the United States Army, combat veteran of Operation Enduring Freedom with the 101st Combat Aviation Brigade, 101st Airborne Division (AASLT) out of Fort Campbell, Kentucky. His other assignments include Fort Rucker, Alabama, where he served as Standardization Instructor Pilot training and evaluating U.S. Army aviators, as well as aviators from the armed forces of Mexico and Colombia. He was also assigned to Joint Task Force Bravo, Soto Cano Air Base, Honduras, where he performed a wide range of missions from counter transnational organized crime, humanitarian assistance/disaster relief all over Central America, South America and the Caribbean. He is currently assigned to the National Training Center (NTC) in Fort Irwin, California.

PREFACE

This is a survival manual that is totally different and hopefully like no other.

It is a collection of knowledge, experience and notes gained over 30 years. Not only by myself, but information gathered from a unique group of friends and professionals that all have experience that needs to be shared, if I miss someone out from the References, it is not my intention so please let me know. This aircrew survival manual is the backbone of some of the skills taught on the HEMS Helicopter Essentials course.

It is aimed specifically at the helicopter aviation industry, those crewmembers that are Non-Pilots and involved in Aeromedical or Rescue operations. I aim to give all helicopter crews, irrespective of their role, underpinning survival knowledge that with practice will allow you to operate safely as a crew and potentially as a basis to improve or develop your own unit protocols, systems and procedures.

This is an aircrew survival manual that encompasses daily routine daily life as well as the worst-case scenario. It covers aspects of the day to day safety culture that is necessary based on experiences from active medical professionals from Heavy Lies the Helmet, IA Med, P1 Air Rescue, UK SAR and active US military special forces aircrew, as well as the traditional survival manuals showing techniques to make fire and shelter.

Some parts may be deemed as controversial, and different to what the reader currently practices. But this is just a small part of the ´just culture´ principles; it will hopefully stimulate critical and active discussion that is an essential ingredient of the flight safety culture. This is not a 'Bible' so to speak, but ideas for you the reader to take onboard and 'set up for success'.

If sections and equipment topics are repeated, it is because they equally apply and need to be repeated, where necessary within the specific chapter context. Please read, enjoy, inwardly digest, disregard or simply pass your time reading in the crew room.

Don´t be a passenger, be part of the whole team…

ACKNOWLEDGEMENTS

Many aircrews, flight medics, nurses and aviation professionals have provided me with valuable knowledge of my past 30 years, and it would be impossible for me to list them all. However, I would like to acknowledge and thank certain people who have supported me in my journey of fulfilling this book: Mario Rene Avila Diaz, my friend and Chief Pilot at Black Wolf Helicopters, Head of Operations Luis Pedro Castillo, Captain Edras Barrera and all Staff at Helicopteros de Guatemala for their never ending patience and willingness to listen to me, Bruno Leoni Luna and Staff at Air Andes Helicopters (Peru), Samuel A Sheldon Jason Stopper at Black Wolf Helicopters (USA), Steve Perry and the awesome staff at StephanH flight clothing, , Alejandro Vargas and Julio Galvezall, the amazing team at Guatefly and 'Wolf 2' currently on active service as a combat helicopter pilot with the US Army.

A special thanks to Michael and Bryan Boone from Heavy Lies the Helmet, Jordan White from After the Call podcast, Chris Smetana at IA Med who have allowed me to forage into the world as a 'Blogger' with the 'Skids up' aviation survival blog, as well as the opportunities to speak on their relevant podcasts as part of the CME collective. Without them, the incentive to produce this manual would never have happened.

Finally, thanks to the Helicopter Association International and BLR Aerospace for having the honor of being the 2019 Salute to Excellence Safety award recipient.

Many of the photographs in this book where not my own were provided by Mario Rene Avila Diaz at Black Wolf, Roberto Diaz and Ronald Garcia from Helicopteros de Guatemala, or Marco Antonio Perez.

CONTENTS

Forward v

Preface ix

Acknowledgements xi

What Kills Us? 1

Risk Management 3

Helicopter Career Pathways 19

Basic Flight Knowledge 32

    Types Of Helicopter And Operational Differences 32

    Common Abbreviations 48

Crew Resource Management 56

    Pre-And Post-Flight Briefings 63

    Preplanning And Mission Planning 66

    Post Mission 71

Survival 77

    ´Dress To Egress´ 80

Protection 116

Location 130

    ´Aviate, Navigate, Communicate´ 134

Water 144

Food 153

Cold Weather And High-Altitude Flights 161

    Dress To Egress 163

Aviation Life Support Equipment (Alse) / Individual Survival Kits 165

Overwater Flights 170

   '3 Seconds Following A Bad Decision' 180

   Cut, Stream, Close And Maintain 194

Putting It All Together 197

Equipment / References 202

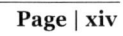

HELICOPTER ESSENTIALS - AIRCREW SURVIVAL MANUAL

WHAT KILLS US?

Helicopters provide an excellent tool, but they have very specific operating limitations, and the consequences of a poorly managed helicopter can be swift and fatal. Furthermore, since helicopters can be extremely dangerous with rotors turning at over 150mph, the hazard to personnel is very real.

All crewmembers need to understand limits and have the professional discipline not to exceed them during an emergency. As accident investigators repeatedly conclude, "self-imposed psychological pressure" causes us to make poor decisions when adrenaline clouds our judgment. Poor decision-making is preventable yet, tragically, it is a factor in many helicopter accidents. You cannot also ignore the fact that a helicopter is a complex machine, they can and do break down, are forced to land and very quickly you may find yourself in a life or death survival situation. This ultimately disrupts operational plans or may leave crews and patients stranded. As part of your planning process, you must include alternative options and extended field care possibilities.

A helicopter is a valuable tool, but not necessarily to be utilized in every situation. Before launching a helicopter for a rescue or requesting the assistance of an outside agency with aviation assets, make sure your decisions are not being driven by the excitement of the moment. Helicopter crews can often show poor judgment by "pressing on" in degraded operating conditions for what is ultimately a non-life-threatening injury that could be managed differently. The option of delaying the mission in favor of safer operating conditions is repeatedly overlooked and requires considerable discipline on the part of a crew.

RISK MANAGEMENT

Survival is defined as the "preservation of one's own life under conditions of immediate peril." To preserve one's own life under adverse conditions requires the ability to live through extreme conditions of emotional and physical shock, and hardship for an indefinite period. Helicopter operations by nature are inherently dangerous, combined with high pressure lifesaving operations, weather and environmental and time – can induce ´immediate peril´.

Survival skills start well before we take off.

Working on the principles of ´knowledge weighs nothing´, if we develop our underlying knowledge of aviation survival principles, we can then augment that with equipment and gear that improves our potential outcome.

Fatigue has often been identified as the 'common denominator' in human factors mishaps because it serves as the 'catalyst' for other human factors to occur. Fatigue can be either acute or chronic. When fatigued, alertness and coordination suffer while performance and judgment become impaired. (ref: U.S.D.O.T. Guidelines for Air-Medical Crew Education, 2001.)

The literature indicates that the best outcomes for the management of fatigue may result from combining multiple strategies; rather than relying on a single strategy. The following basic guiding principles relate to both general and specific environments (i.e.; road /helicopter):

Aircrew should always present themselves well rested and fit for duty at the commencement of shift.

Dispatch Staff should consider the clinical urgency of missions when tasking crews on missions that have significant chance of causing or increasing crew fatigue and where reasonable transfers should take place during daylight hours.

Individuals should take into consideration 'I.M.S.A.F.E' which list all the key factors that impact on fatigue:

>**I**llness
>
>**M**edication
>
>**S**tress
>
>**A**lcohol
>
>**F**atigue
>
>**E**at

We have all probably heard this being used, but what does it mean? Most are straight forward, but the three people most often misunderstand are:

1. **Illness** – If we have a headache, feel 'under the weather', have a cold so that our sinuses are blocked an we are unable to clear pressure differences in our ears. All these affect our ability to clearly think and make good decisions whilst maintaining all round situational awareness.

2. **Medication** – FAR 91.17 prohibits the use of "any drug that affects the persons faculties in any way contrary to safety. These include, but aren't limited to, anticoagulants, antiviral agents, anxiolytics (anti-anxiety), barbiturates, chemotherapeutic agents, experimental, hypoglycaemic, investigational, mood altering, motion sickness, narcotic, sedating, antihistaminic, steroids, or tranquilizers. Whilst there isn't a definite list provided by the FAA for example, there is a lot of guidance available on Aviation Administration websites.

3. **Stress** – Everyday for most of us! This more refers to the increased cardiovascular output caused by excessive WORKLOAD. Why CRM uses checklists…

4. **Alcohol** – In the USA, Commercial airline pilots have a blood alcohol concentration limit of 0.04, which is half that of driving a car. The general rule is '8 hours bottle to throttle', although most companies increase this to 12 hours. A key point the UK military

introduced as I was leaving was that the Military Police could/ would randomly breathalyse anyone involved in flight operations. This included the MAINTAINERS, Why? We can all be sober, but if Smudge Smith the mechanic is still drunk and doing pre-flight maintenance...

5. **Fatigue** – who isn't tired? Fatigue is a fact of life; it's how we manage it. All legislation and guidance include paragraphs of fatigue management, some of the more common points that your unit needs to address are:

> 5.1 **Preventive strategies** should be used before and between duty periods. Try to get the best possible sleep before duty time and avoid starting shifts with sleep debt, where possible. Try to get 8 hours sleep per 24-hour period. "Anchor sleep" during your usual sleep time should be maintained if possible
>
> 5.2 **Good sleep habits** are a second countermeasure strategy. Develop and practice a pre-sleep routine. If hungry, eat a light snack, but do not eat or drink heavily before sleeping. Use physical or mental relaxation techniques and sleep in a room that is dark, quiet and at comfortable temperature. If you don't fall asleep in 30 minutes, get out of bed. The use of "white noise" can mask external sounds. Exercise regularly, but not too near sleep periods.
>
> 5.3 **Operational strategies** to maintain alertness during duty periods are varied but may include; physical activity and conversation with others. Balanced nutrition is also necessary for alertness. The brain needs a steady fuel supply to operate. Avoid simple carbohydrates that cause peaks of insulin release. Instead, consume complex carbohydrates and proteins. Stay well hydrated, since mental functions are the first to be affected by dehydration. Thirst is not a sensitive indicator of dehydration. Urine output and color is the best indicator of hydration status.
>
> 5.4 **Strategic napping** during duty periods, the 'NASA nap', is another operational strategy. Extensive NASA research clearly demonstrates the effectiveness of brief naps in improving performance. A planned and

coordinated brief 'NASA nap' up to 45 minutes in duration is helpful if operations permit.

6. **Eat** – This is not a medical book; you are all professionals and will know of the effects of hypoglycaemia. Not eating = bad decisions.

More importantly is hydration!

In a study by Omni Medical Systems, they found that 'The practice of "tactical dehydration" – pilots avoiding the consumption of liquids for hours before missions, in order to avoid in-flight bladder relief, is widespread in military aviation'.

In the same studies they cite that the effects of an aircrew member having a full bladder

A Joint Staff (J-39) "Review of Effects of Heat Stress and Potential Correlation on Mishaps in the CENTCOM Theatre of Operations" iv cited research findings that "visual motor tracking, short-term memory, attention, and arithmetic efficiency were all impaired at 2% dehydration [while] 4% dehydration effects a 23% increase in response time (in comparison, a .08 Blood Alcohol Content level [legally "impaired" in all 50 states] yields a 17% increase in response time). This argues that the operational risks of tactical dehydration may be greater than those of intoxication.

So, in plain language – DRINK!

GAR (Green-Amber-Red) Model - Risk Assessment

The GAR model allows for time critical risk assessment and generates <u>communication</u> concerning the mission risks. This communication then helps identify the risk and leads to the appropriate mitigation. The GAR model can be applied in a variety of situations. It can be used to help identify programmatic risk and is efficient enough to be utilized as a pre-mission risk assessment tool. The GAR model is not intended to replace pre-mission planning, briefings and debriefings, or post action follow-up, but to provide an efficient risk management tool for dynamic environments.

Making risk decisions at the appropriate level establishes clear accountability. Those accountable for the success or failure of a mission must be included in the risk decision process. The higher the risk the more mitigation may be necessary. If significant difference in the same rating categories are identified all team members will re-evaluate the mission and address any mitigation prior to continuing with the mission.

It provides a more general analysis of the operational system and provides a qualitative rating scale for each of the categories that correspond to the identified areas of risk. It is important to remember that risk management is a process that continues throughout the mission and each assessment model allows management to set the acceptable risk standards as they apply to each mission.

The GAR model should be applied to helicopter rescue missions as appropriate. All helicopter crew shall receive training on the GAR model and its use. The senior Aircrewman shall be responsible for implementing the GAR model with all members of the team.

A GAR Risk Assessment model, which creates a GO/NO-GO decision tool, will be conducted individually by each member of the Team prior to initial dispatch on the Operational/Mission Risk Assessment Worksheet (attached). Individual scores will be compiled on the Crewman/Manager Assessment Worksheet and reviewed and discussed by all members of the Team. Mitigation if any will be discussed and documented on the Worksheet. The assessment may be completed at the beginning of an operational period but must be reviewed and updated if the team or mission changes or other mission-specific information becomes available. The

Team is made up of the Crewman, IC, Pilot, and Ops Manager. If assigned to a Large Incident the Helibase Manager or Equivalent will be considered an essential team member.

Operations that have a total post mitigation score in the amber range can be conducted with pilot and crewman concurrence. Rescue operations with a post mitigation score in the red will need line officer or IC approval to proceed with the mission.

Risk Control Categories

Supervision

Supervisory Control considers how qualified the supervisor is and whether effective supervision is taking place. Supervision acts as a control to minimize risk. The higher the risk, the more the supervisor needs to be focused on observing and checking. A supervisor who is actively involved in a task is easily distracted and should not be considered an effective safety observer in moderate to high-risk conditions.

Planning

Planning and Communication should consider how much information you, your team, and other resources with whom you may be interacting have: Does everyone have the same information? How accurate is the information? Is there adequate time to plan for and evaluate the existing and emerging conditions? What is the availability of contingency resources and how reliable is the communication infrastructure? Can effective CRM be established with this information?

Team Selection

Team selection for the stated mission should consider the knowledge, skills, proficiency, and competence of the individuals. Team fitness should consider the physical and mental state of the crew to include the rescue team, medics, crewman, pilot, and helicopter. The amount and quality of duty/rest a team member has had as well as an evaluation of all internal and external stress are important factors to consider.

Environment

Consider area of operation that would influence performance of the aircraft to include but not limited to; density altitude, temperature, wind, topography, etc. Known factors such as terrain, forest canopy, site selection should be eyed with caution as the operational environment is very dynamic.

Incident Complexity

Evaluate the experience level of the team. Generally, the longer one is exposed to a hazard, the greater are the risks. The situation includes considering how long the environmental conditions will remain stable and the complexity of the work.

Supervision

Supervisor has perfect knowledge about the mission, personnel, capabilities and limitations, and is able to apply the appropriate control to minimize risk

1 – 2 – 3 – 4 – 5

Supervisor has little knowledge about the mission, personnel, capabilities and limitations, and lacks skill, knowledge or ability to apply the appropriate control to minimize risk.

Planning

There is a well-designed plan that is reviewed and revised as needed to meet the demands for safety and efficiency and to account for adaption. Time is well managed. CRM is in place and well versed on with all parties.

Adequate personnel and technology are available to relay information accurately to those who make the decisions. Contingency personnel, resources, and equipment are readily available.

1 – 2 – 3 – 4 – 5

There is no plan, or the plan doesn't

address many current adaptations made in response of demands for efficiency.

Time constraints have a strong effect on ability to plan. CRM is poor or not utilized. Communications are poor between personnel. Communication equipment is lacking efficiency and coverage of response area. No contingency personnel, resources, or equipment.

Team Selection

Multiple personnel are trained, proficient, healthy, and rested prior to starting the mission. Personal

1 – 2 – 3 – 4 – 5

Only one person is available and the success of the mission depends on that person juggling

issues are addressed, and little external stress is being exerted. Selection and preparation are done well in advance so there is plenty of time for personnel to get personal and job-related demands addressed.

many responsibilities to squeeze this mission into the work schedule. Personnel lack training.

Personnel have been squeezing in many additional duties as assigned distracting them from their proficiency or personal life.

Environment

Weather and visibility are conducive to the best possible chance for success in the mission. Operational tempo is appropriate for the mission.

1 – 2 – 3 – 4 – 5

Winds are unpredictable, temperature is extreme, low ceilings and visibilities, precipitation, sun angle creates strong shadows, etc. Mission tempo is too low or high.

Mission Complexity

A single agency is involved with personnel from the same unit who regularly work together. Mission is straight forward and covered by standard operating procedures. Non-medical emergency operation.

1 – 2 – 3 – 4 – 5

Multiple agencies are involved in a mission that defies definition or has ever been attempted. Personnel are new to each other and come from different cultures. Many leaders are emerging and working toward different objectives. Numerous resources responding.

Daily Operational/Mission Risk Assessment Worksheet

GREEN	AMBER	RED	CREW	IC	PILOT	BASE MANAGER	*TEAM-MITIGATIONN SCORE
0 - 11	12 - 19	20 - 25					
Risk rated 1-5 for each category. Mitigations should be considered for any category rated higher than 3. If 1 or more categories' rate higher than 3, a team-mitigation needs to be completed for that category. A team-mitigation will also have to be completed if the total of the individual score is greater than 12.							
Supervision: Presence, accessibility and effectiveness of leadership for all teams and personnel. Clear chain of command.							
Planning: Adequate briefings and mission planning time available. Shared communications plan. Radio communications available throughout area of operations.							

Team Selection: Level of individual training and experience. Level of team member's rest/fatigue, physical fitness, morale, and absence of outside distractions. All team member's current in required qualifications and standardized procedures.				
Environment: Extreme temperatures, elevation, difficulty of terrain (aspect, canopy, slope, etc.), long approach, remoteness.				
Incident Complexity: Potential for incident that would tax the current staffing levels. Potential for large fire growth or medical response. Severity and probability of mishap.				
Total				

GREEN	AMBER	RED
0 - 11	12 – 19	20 - 25
LOW RISK	**MODERATE RISK**	**HIGH RISK**
Proceed With Mission	**Proceed With Caution**	**Implement measures Prior to Proceeding**

*The team-mitigation column would be used if any one team member's overall score goes into the amber or red, or if an individual rate any category higher than a 3. Mitigation measures *will be documented on the following page. If the team's consensus mitigation score stays in the red, they will need Line Officer or IC approval to proceed* with the mission.

The ability to assign numerical values or "color codes" to hazards is not the most important part of risk assessment. Team discussion is critical to understanding the risks and how they will be managed.

Crew/Team Mitigations:

IC/Line officer Signature:

Planning considerations

Intelligence gathering is a key first step in mission planning. Time spent planning is time well spent.

Mission planning should include:

- Mission type (Rescue, point of injury, Inter facility?)
- Equipment required
- The mission plan
- Support/ Back up units
- Communications plan
- Contingency/ Emergency plans

Intelligence Gathering – G.R.A.D.E		
G	Gather information	Source all available information related to the mission (e.g.; reports from scene, photos, weather reports, maps, local knowledge, internet searches etc)
R	Review for relevance	Focus on relevant information only
A	Analyse alternatives	Consider possible alternatives (e.g.; non-rope response, cancel or delay mission etc)
D	Determine priorities	Set order of priorities (e.g.; most to least important)
E	Execute	Conduct operation and constantly review (e.g.; document good and bad points)

Mission Plan – T.S.M.E.A.C. S

T	**Topography**	Description of the terrain, geography & environment the mission is being conducted in
S	**Situation**	Statement of what the current situation is
M	**Mission**	Clear explanation of the goal
E	**Execution**	Step by step list of how the mission is going to be performed
A	**Administration & Logistics**	Description of equipment/gear to be used, job delegations & contingency plans
C	**Command & Signals**	Chain of Command, communication methods and timings
S	**Safety**	Identified hazards & specific requirements

Mission plans must be communicated to the whole crew and the Operations Room, as a minimum. Updates to the mission plan should be communicated as appropriate to all those involved in the planning process.

Planning Resources

A range of planning resources are available to assist:

- Operations Staff/ Local Knowledge
- Specialist Guidebooks
- Flight Clinical Care Manager

Four Key Questions (4W):

These can be used to provide a basic framework for a mission plan. For example, you are in mid air and get diverted from a training mission to an actual incident.

1. What? *(Has happened)*
2. Where? *(Has it happened – Exact location)*
3. When? *(What time did it happen)*
4. Who? *(Who is involved, numbers and were they prepared)*

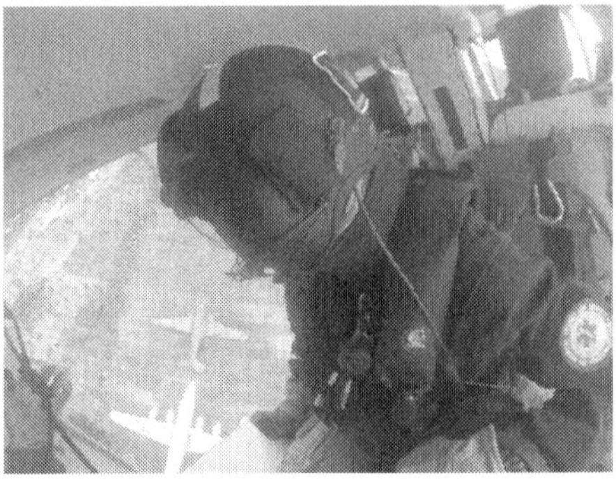

HELICOPTER CAREER PATHWAYS

Helicopter career pathways

Getting into a Helicopter team is not easy.

But not impossible.

The aim of this chapter is to introduce the different ways of achieving this type of work. It does not include the helicopter pilots that are predominantly ex-military and have strict pre-requirements before any companies look at taking them on.

The global helicopter aircrew community is actually very small, with most progressing from a military or coastguard aircrew/ rescue career into the civilian sector. In most parts of the world, helicopter SAR services are only provided by the military, coastguard or the larger commercial helicopter operators (for example CHC, Bond helicopters). These companies usually recruit only trained and experienced aircrew and technicians, however, with (for example) the UK military handing over SAR services solely to the private sector, career opportunities globally are being offered. Some of these jobs are often ´dual role´ so one day you would be the hoist operator, the second day the rescue technician. This system is designed to prevent skill loss and enhance crew coordination, although dependent on the skill level of the medical crew used, is nowadays becoming rarer due to the impossibilities of maintaining currency in both roles.

For the ´rest of the world´, this leaves three very distinct roles: Aircrew or Flight Medic and SAR Technicians.

Aircrewman / Helicopter Rescue Officer

Not to be confused with the term ´Crew Chief´ (who is an aircraft maintainer initially, later trained for flight duties), the Aircrewman is not a maintainer, but is also directly responsible to the pilot for everything that happens inside, underneath and outside the helicopter. As an example to be qualified in this trade in the military as a profession takes on average 1 year, with extensive training in navigation, weather, fuel and weight calculations, aerodynamics, refueling, plus ,more – everything the same as the pilots learn, but without the flying part. It can be achieved through the civilian sector (at a considerable cost if not sponsored) with a few companies offering training. The key though in choosing is looking at not only the course content – but how many FLIGHT HOURS you receive.

For example, a training school offers:

3 weeks of theoretical and practical training on, leveraging largely on the use of our virtual reality Complete Aircrew Training Simulator (CATS), enabling more efficient learning in a stress-less environment.

The Course is a full-time course conducted over a period of 15 days at the Training Centre.

During this course, you will attend:

- 47 hours of theoretical training;
- 22 hours in simulators, CATS (Complete Aircrew Training System), Dry Winch and HUET
- 2 hours of actual flying

So, for approximately $15,000 you receive only 22 simulator and 2 actual flying hours... Simulator hours are fantastic to teach drills, procedures in a safe environment, but do not expect to walk into an Aircrewman position on completion. The aim of these courses is to give you the fundamentals which you then develop during flight operations.

For job applications, an industry standard usually requires a minimum of 500 hours after training.

This is an example of company requirements for an aircrew position:

Aircrewmen Requirements

Essential Requirements

- Possess a current class 1 drivers license
- Be over 18yrs of age at time of selection
- Be in possession of a current Senior first Aid Certificate
- Have completed the Advanced Resuscitation Certificate (current)
- Flight Radiotelephone operators License (current)
- Hoist endorsement in accordance with C.A.O. 29:11
- Minimum 500hrs aircrew experience
- Pass WHRS physical fitness test ***

Desirable Experience and Qualifications

- SAR/EMS Experience
- Bell 412 / BK 117 experience
- Helicopter Underwater Escape Training (H.U.E.T)

There are NO shortcuts. Aviation regulations and the industry itself require you to have certification and recognized standard skills and knowledge.

So, where does that leave you? If it is a profession that you wish to pursue, find the helicopter company that you want to work for, and go and ask, speak to the crew and see what they think is the best way forward.

If in a remote region, or if you ask nicely, go and offer to work in the hangar, so that you start becoming comfortable around helicopters, you then may progress to working out on the ramp / apron – moving helicopters around, helping load luggage for passengers, participating with underslung load work / rigging etc.

Whatever you do – keep a log! And get it signed / stamped! The advantage of doing this allows the regular crews to learn your NAME.

As mentioned earlier, the helicopter world is very small, and vacancies are often ´who you know´.

All these hours show your ability to work in an aviation environment. Then, look at a course to give you the basic aircrew skills, where you will get further flight hours. Step by step your proficiency will increase, look at doing an aviation survival course, underwater egress training, CRM, increase your medical training (remember many positions are dual role) in your own time.

Some companies (especially in Australia) operate a voluntary crewman position. Not specifically as the crewman, but as part of the total crew, yes you don´t get paid, but you get trained and accrue hours for free!

Courses usually progress from Basic, Intermediate, Advanced and then specialist techniques.

Don´t immediately go out and pay for a ´Advanced hoist operator's course with Night Vision Devices´ - yes you will learn a lot, but without the foundation knowledge will be a waste of your money. Leave that course for when you need it (and hopefully when you do – somebody else will pay for it for you!), for example a <u>basic</u> hoist course (6 days) can cost in the region of $24,000! But hoist operations are only a small part of the tradecraft of an Aircrewman.

Ask questions:

- What will the course give me?
- Am I getting value for money?
- Are my job prospects realistic once I finish the course?
- Is the training provider making claims and promises perhaps they can't keep?
- Is it nationally accredited training? Many training companies offer accreditation certificates through colleges/ universities – not always needed as usually a certificate from a helicopter includes the signature of a ´Certified Flight Instructor´.

Remember most reputable organizations will require an Aircrewman to have a minimum of 500hrs before they get even a look in. That is 500hrs of experience related to the job you are applying for.

As an employer it is highly unlikely, I would employ an Aircrewman/ winch operator fresh off a course. An Aircrewman needs to be able to operate independently in the back and they require a wealth of knowledge and experience in order to do that.

Think the following scenario – *Its nighttime, adverse weather in the mountains or overwater, with multiple survivors to rescue. You must coordinate with the Pilot, the rescue crewman plus all the other associated tasks to achieve a safe mission.*

Would ten hours combined simulator and flight training give you the skills and confidence to deal with that?

Be realistic on what you will achieve if you are thinking on paying $1000's of dollars. These training companies will be happy to take your cash and promise the world, read the fine print.

Used the internet, look at the common requirements for vacancies, and simply work through the list. Then like any job application, it's what you can do to make your application stand out. Start small and become an efficient and safe crewman, progress to hoist and rescue operations when in a company that will provide the training to you.

Rescue Crewman / SAR Technician

Not all companies operate dual role positions and specialist rescue personnel are used utilized commonly by helicopter operators. This is often the case where helicopters are not fitted with hoists.

Whether this is as a permanent member of the helicopter crew or as an asset that can be drawn upon due to your specific area knowledge and skill set. The advantage of using 'Rescue Paramedics' (for example), is that ultimately the medical care delivered to a patient is increased dramatically.

Rescue crewman are normally either land based (only) or water / land operations. Those that operate overwater usually have a minimum swimming and lifesaving standard that is required to apply for a vacancy, in order to make sure that you are safe to enter the water. Crew fitness testing standards are usually similar across the world and may include (as a minimum):

- Run 2.4 km in 12 minutes
- Swim 500 meters in 11 minutes [wearing fins, wetsuit & harness]
- Patient recovery swim, 300 meters in 10 minutes [wearing fins, wetsuit & harness]. This comprises a 50-meter swim, dive to bottom of pool, recover patient & return with patient 50 meters (must be completed 3 times)
- Strength: 30 sit-ups, 20 push-ups, 10 second arm flex (hold weight with elbows bent to 90 degrees only. Knees raised to 90 degrees perpendicular to torso)
- Survival: 12 minutes tread water in flight suit/overalls (initial applicants only)
- Total time: the test must be completed in entirety within a 2-hour window.

Intensive selection processes then take place, once successful, the helicopter provider trains you internally specifically to their Standard Operating Procedures.

Some of the knowledge and skills necessary for joint land/ water operations are:

- Sea survival
- Helicopter Underwater Escape
- Sea and open water operations
- Rescue swimmer and white-water winching operations

- Vessel winching and boat access
- SAR Equipment and specialized rescue operations
- Land winching including stretchers and strops
- Patient access and management in remote areas
- All terrain operations (Mountain, alpine, forest and desert operations)
- Working within a multi crew team

For the medical professional, the skills apply your medical background and profession in an austere environment specific to the mission needs. The Rescue team manager and aircrew need to be confident that YOU can survive the environment you are put into. The ´hierarchy of rescue´ mentioned in other chapters - ´the rescuer, NEVER, needs rescuing´.

Helicopters are fantastic; however, the need fuel are susceptible to weather and may one day have to leave you on the ground for their own safety. This is a situation that is avoided at all costs, but a reality that must be prepared for as part of the risk mitigation process.

As a guide on the skills necessary to not only be safe in and around the aircraft, but an actual asset that needs to be utilized, these are the minimum qualifications required by all the Flight Medics utilized by Black Wolf Helicopters

- High School Diploma;
- Nationally Registered EMT;
- PHTLS (Pre-Hospital Trauma Life Support);
- NAEMT Tactical Combat Casualty Care;
- Basic Cardiac Life Support (BCLS);
- Advanced Cardiac Life Support (ACLS);

- Pediatric Advanced Life Support (PALS);
- Wilderness EMT (upgrade);
- NAEMT All Hazards Disaster Response;
- ICS/ Triage;
- Aircraft Human External Cargo (winch / short haul);
- Helicopter abseil / rappel;
- Helicopter Underwater Escape Training;
- Survival and Aviation Life Support Equipment (ALSE);
- Participation in internal programs to maintain currency of skills and knowledge.

A lot of qualifications? The aims of these minimums are to ensure that the rescue team has the ability not only to care for their patient, but also themselves. It allows them to have the skill set to be put into any situation and be effective. Part of this process is also the minimum equipment that they individually carry as standard, to augment their training.

As a medical professional, many will have the majority of these already. It is now a case of augmenting the ´usual´ medical qualifications with those specific to wilderness or austere environments, as well as the more specialist rescue/ technical skills (that allow you to rescue the patient).

These courses may include:

- Crew Resource Management;
- Rope Rescue Technician;
- Swiftwater Rescue Technician;

- Search management and planning
- Missing person behavior
- Extended Casualty Care

The goal is to prepare you to be physically and mentally to be able to manage a scene safely, assess and treat patients, rescue where necessary and provide clear, concise instructions to additional assets that need to know.

To summarize, pathways into these specialized roles are long and potentially complex. Outside of the military or a sponsored program they can be very expensive, but with correct planning and preparation, they are careers that can be achieved.

Logbooks

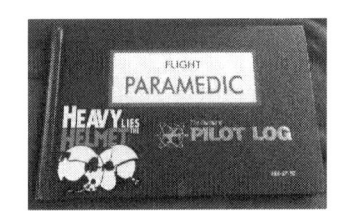

What many crews fail to do however, is keep a record. Pilots do it, so should we. Why?

1. It is a personal record for either your own memory purposes, or for future generations
2. It is a record that if signed and stamped can presented as part of any job application
3. For this transitioning from a military flying career to civilian, is a record of all the skills that you possess

Firstly, you need to understand how helicopter timings are written as aviation generally uses a system that you may not be familiar with. Rotor time is gained from the pilot after each flight according to the aircraft Hobbs meter (or similar).

Times are expressed for example as 0.4 (zero point four), 1.2 (one point two)

0.1 hours = 6 minutes.

For example;

- 0.3 hours = 18 minutes.
- 1.0 = 60 minutes.

So, then all we need to do is record the following:

Date / Helicopter tail number / where from and to / hours / what you were doing.

Logbooks for crewmembers are not normally standardized, so as long as that is your minimum information then you are good to go. I do know some rescue guys that keep newspaper clippings in the page for jobs that have a poignant memory etc

I just use a standard pilot's logbook and amend the headings as required.

Left page:

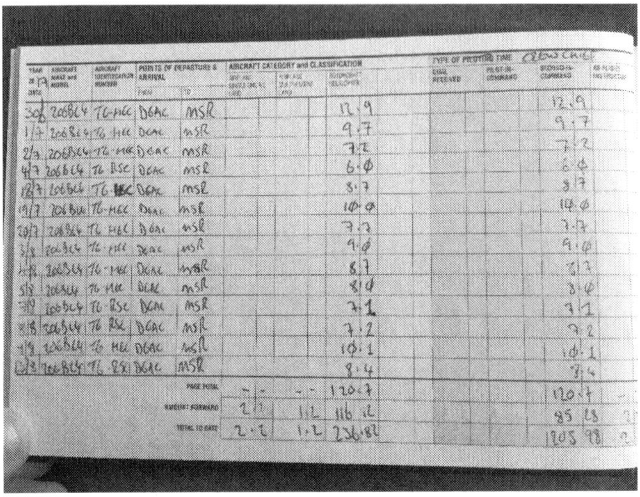

Right page:

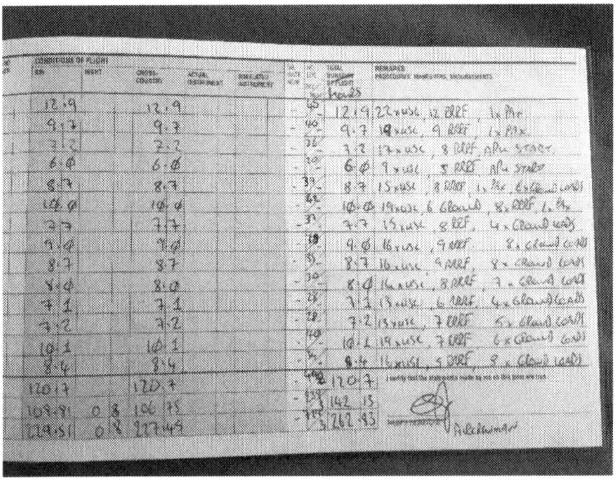

At the end of each month you self-certify and can get a few pilots signatures / your Chief Pilots signature every quarter just to confirm authenticity.

I also include any aviation safety, survival or mandatory ground schools and specialist refreshers that I do. These are then signed by whoever the CFI (Certified Flight Instructor) is for that check test.

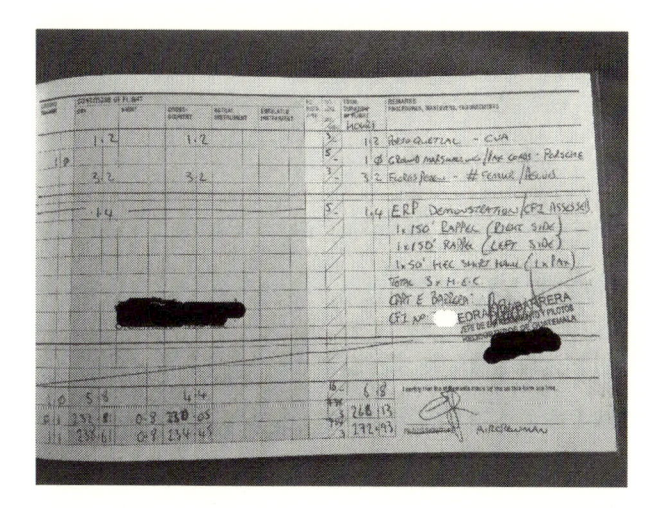

For those who wish to pursue a career in aviation, remember that it is a marathon, not a sprint, persistence beats resistance. The more you try, the luckier you will be.

BASIC FLIGHT KNOWLEDGE

Types of helicopter and operational differences

The Incident Command System has four classifications of helicopters, which are similar to the "Light," "Medium," and "Heavy" classifications used in the past.

- A Type I helicopter seats at least 16 people and has a minimum capacity of 5,000 lbs. Both a CH-47 (Chinook) and UH-60 (Blackhawk) are Type I helicopters.

- A Type II helicopter seats at least 10 people and has a minimum capacity of 2,500 lbs. Both an UH1-H and a Bell 212 are Type II helicopters.

- A Type III helicopter seats at least 5 people and has a minimum capacity of 1,200 lbs. Both a 206 and a Hughes 500 are Type III helicopters.

- A Type IV helicopter seats at least 3 people and has a minimum capacity of 600 lbs.

The first and safest method of insertion and extraction of casualties will always be landing the helicopter normally. Contrary to popular belief, helicopters do not routinely take off vertically; because of power limitations, they require forward flight to gain lift.

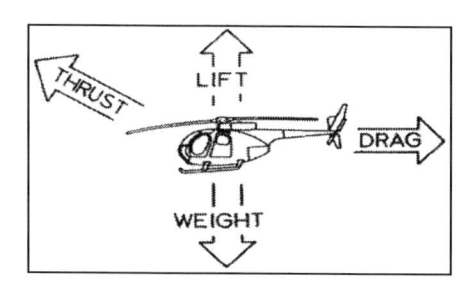

In developing countries or where crews utilize local services (for example the use of Sherriff Department helicopters in United States), many helicopters are not fitted with a hoist / winch and other insertion / extraction techniques are utilized.

Helicopters can make pickups in three ways:

1. Landing at a Helicopter Landing Site (HLS) / Landing Zone (LZ),
2. By making a hovering or one-skid recovery, or
3. By using an external load operation (hoists, short hauls)

The last two are hazardous, even under optimal conditions. In conditions of mountainous terrain, evacuations should be by landing if possible, even if this means a trail carry of the victim by ground crews to a nearby HLS. In many mountainous rescue situations, there is plenty of time to locate or construct a safe HLS rather than try hovering or one-skid recoveries.

Dependent on the size of helicopter, improvised Helicopter Landing Sites (HLS) can vary in size. If you are unaware of the type of helicopter that is assisting you, as a rough guide they need to be at least 100ft x 100ft (similar size to a football pitch, with no obstructions.

Helicopter Crews use the ´5 S´s and discuss the wind´ in the following format when identifying potential landing sites:

- WIND – Direction and Strength ('wind direction' is the direction the wind comes from).
- SIZE – Ideally as big as a football pitch.
- SHAPE – Note the shape (this will also aid in air to ground identification).
- SURROUNDINGS – Ideally no wires, pylons, trees or buildings (including the approach path and 'overshoot')
- SURFACES – If boggy or wet inform the Pilot. The ground should be able to support a 4x4 Landrover sized vehicle without sinking. Check for loose articles, debris, personal clothing and kit.
- SLOPE – As level as possible.

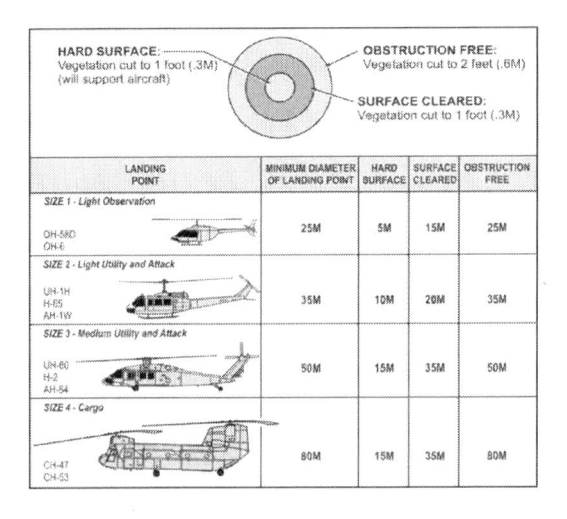

LANDING POINT	MINIMUM DIAMETER OF LANDING POINT	HARD SURFACE	SURFACE CLEARED	OBSTRUCTION FREE
SIZE 1 - Light Observation OH-58D OH-6	25M	5M	15M	25M
SIZE 2 - Light Utility and Attack UH-1H H-65 AH-1W	35M	10M	20M	35M
SIZE 3 - Medium Utility and Attack UH-60 H-2 AH-64	50M	15M	35M	50M
SIZE 4 - Cargo CH-47 CH-53	80M	15M	35M	80M

HARD SURFACE: Vegetation cut to 1 foot (.3M) (will support aircraft)
OBSTRUCTION FREE: Vegetation cut to 2 feet (.6M)
SURFACE CLEARED: Vegetation cut to 1 foot (.3M)

Search and Rescue Operations

Helicopter Search and Rescue (SAR) operations involve highly specialized and trained aircrews with many hours of training and in most cases specially designed helicopters available to operate in all weathers 24/7. Most SAR helicopters rely extensively on the use of a hoist / winch and utilize a crew of four: Pilot in Command, Co-Pilot, and a rear crew consisting of a Winch Operator and Winchman (responsible for ´down the wire´ operations). In European theatres of operations, the rear crews are usually both registered Paramedics (to allow crew rotation), in other countries the Winchman is usually an EMT and the hoist operator / crew chief first aid trained (due to the different work profile). Ground units/ Rescue teams usually have very little inter-action with this type of helicopter operation, in some areas this is limited to transporting Mountain Rescue Teams into (or out of) search areas as these types of helicopters operate independently and are a totally self-sufficient asset.

Landing Recoveries

Hazards exist even in relatively safe conditions of a landing recovery whereby the helicopter will normally come to full rotor stop. The casualty should be briefed regarding helicopter safety, including a warning to stay away from the rear of the helicopter, especially the tail rotor, always. Even if the helicopter is fully without power, rescuers should escort any walking casualty to the helicopter and assure that they are secured in their seat with their full seat belt, including chest harness.

The rescuer should always anticipate that the helicopter flight will make the casualty nauseous and should be prepared for the possibility that the casualty may vomit during the transport.

Helicopter Safety Zones

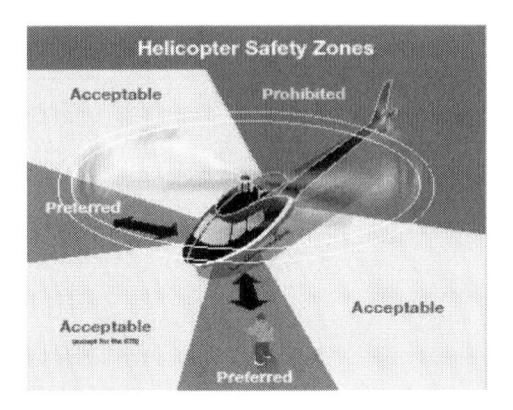

At all times the personnel should be aware of helicopter danger areas, and follow these golden rules:

- Clear HLS of loose articles. Secure your gear from the effects of rotor wash.

Do not approach without receiving a visual signal from the Pilot / Rear Crewman. Never leave without a visual or spoken instruction to do so. Stay where the pilot can always see you.

Crouch while walking for extra rotor clearance. Always remove hats. Never reach up or chase after anything that blows away.

Fasten and adjust your seat belt on entering the helicopter and leave it fastened until the Pilot/Rear Crewman signals you to get out.

Never approach or leave a helicopter when its engine and rotors are running down or starting up.

On sloping ground always approach or leave on the downslope side for maximum rotor clearance.

If you are blinded by swirling dust or grit or get disorientated, STOP – crouch lower, or sit down and wait for assistance.

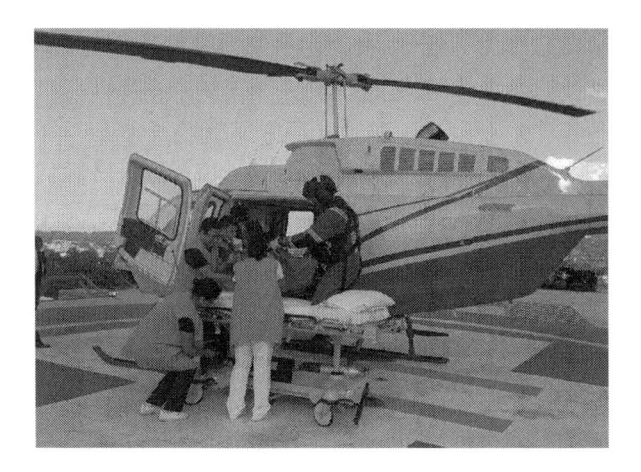

'Mast Bumping'

Certain helicopters have two-bladed, "semi-rigid" blades. When one blade flaps up, the other flaps down. The connection part of the down-flapping rotor blade can knock against or 'bump' the rotor mast. The rotor mast being the main shaft of the rotor blades. Helicopters have hard rubber and metal protectors to reduce wear if possible, but this bumping can cause fractures within the metal. If a fracture occurs on the rotor shaft, what happens? The rotor blades fall off – not a good day!

It can happen in flight with excessive cyclic input from the pilot in certain conditions. But that's why he is the Pilot, as Crewmembers, we are limited to supporting the pilot during high wind start-ups. As stated, this is for semi-rigid style rotor heads, so wont affect everybody, but our task is simple.

We hold the rotor blade in our hand until the engine has enough power to pull it out of our hand. Yes, we hold the rotor blade.

This allows the greater torque delivered by the turbine to immediately apply centrifugal forces and prevent the blades 'bumping'. Pictured is a RNZAF UH-1 (female) rear crew doing this:

Hovering and One-Skid Recoveries

In certain situation, pilots and rescuers may choose to perform a hovering (where the helicopter remains at full power on or above the ground) or one-skid recovery of a rescue victim. In this case, serious medical complications are likely present, which warrants the more hazardous recovery.

Medical problems of a casualty can be compromised during hovering or one-skid recoveries, due to fear, uncertainty and anxiety. Rescuers should advise the casualty what will happen prior to the actual helicopter pickup. They must be certain that the casualty can withstand the strain of the recovery procedures, which will include very high noise levels combined with high rotor wash and dangerous conditions.

If rescuers do not have communications with the pilot and the rescuer will not accompany the casualty on board the helicopter, a patient card should be attached to the casualty stating the medical condition and treatment given (example: ATMIST Format) as well as where s/he is to be taken.

The factors to be taken into account in selecting a site for a hovering recovery are generally the same as those for selecting a HLS. In these conditions, a smaller ground area, rougher terrain and steeper slope are permissible. On the other hand, it is extremely important that there be plenty of room for both the main rotor and the tail rotor boom, since the pilot may have to turn the helicopter in the event changes in wind direction.

An experienced Marshaller, one that the pilot knows is competent, should be at the site and all ground personnel should be within the pilot's view, if possible. In the case of one-skid recoveries on rock outcrops, this may be impractical.

One of the techniques you will commonly hear used is ´Short Haul´. To define simply, to transport one or more persons suspended beneath a helicopter, this is also referred to by the aviation term simply as ´HEC´ (human external cargo) from the operational procedures for external cargo loads. Hoist operations, fast rope, rappelling to name a few are all Human External Cargo operations and are all governed by specific aviation standards.

The FAA defines a helicopter load as:

´An external load is defined as a load that is carried or extends outside the aircraft fuselage. An external load may include, but not be limited to, persons on the skids (including helocasting. and single skid operations involving loading or unloading of the helicopter) and/or a load attached to the cargo hook or rescue hoist. It includes the attaching hardware and the load´.

History

Helicopter Short Haul operations were originally researched and developed by the Swiss Air Rescue Service (REGA) in 1966, in 1970 National Parks Canada adopted and incorporated Helicopter Short Haul into their own Search and Rescue program, where it continues to be widely used to this day. By 1980 helicopter short haul was adopted and modified by a variety of agencies within the United States of America and continues to be an effective and safe tool to meet various agencies operational objectives.

The development of the short-haul technique has been closely associated with the evolution of helicopter rappelling. When ground evacuation was dangerous or impractical, personnel were removed from rappel sites by attaching to rappel lines that were anchored to the helicopter. While helicopter rappel requires extended hover time for the delivery of persons to a specific location, short haul emphasizes limited hover time with added capability of the extraction of persons and cargo.

In Short Haul, the helicopter hovers above the casualty, who is secured to the line by ground personnel. When the casualty (usually accompanied by a trained rescuer) is secured, the helicopter gains altitude, lifting the casualty off the ground. Since the victim is suspended, the helicopter simply transports the casualty to a predetermined area where other ground personnel will disconnect the casualty from the system once the victim is on the ground.

A mission specific training program will introduce you to safe helicopter operations and provide the necessary training to be classed as a 'Short Hauler'.

Short haulers must:

i. Have completed Helicopter Safety Training.

ii. Demonstrate knowledge of the inspection, care and maintenance of short-haul equipment and rigging.

iii. Demonstrate knowledge of short-haul procedures.

iv. Demonstrate knowledge of emergency procedures.

v. Complete a minimum of two short-hauls without procedural error (Training should include receiving equipment/ cargo).

vi. Demonstrate knowledge of risk assessment and mission components.

Flight Restrictions

A. Short Haul Flight operations and procedures should only be conducted from ½ hour before official sunrise until ½ hour after official sunset, or during extended twilight hours when terrain features can be readily distinguishable for a distance of at least one mile. Additionally, hand signals from the short-haulers, ground crew and the aircrew must be clearly visible.

B. Visibility for short-haul missions shall be a minimum of ½ mile (VFR).

PPE Standards

Personal Protective Equipment (PPE) is always required to be worn during Helicopter Operations.

The following is the minimum equipment required; however, additional items may be added to increase the Short Haulers safety. The manufacturer's recommendations for proper use should be taught and be followed.

Helmets, Ear and Eye Protection

All short haulers are required to wear a helmet, protective eye wear and ear plugs (Energy Absorbent Resin (EAR) or similar)

Footwear

Short haulers may utilize footwear that is appropriate for mission safety, this may include mountaineering boots, safety boots etc. Whatever the design, they should fully enclose the toe and heel of the short hauler and be of a lace design.

Harnesses

All short haulers will wear a commercially made harness that adheres to one or more of the local/ national standards. In order to prevent the unlikely event of inversion, and for a better seating position, a full body harness is generally better. Do not over tighten the leg/ thigh straps though, this allows you to adjust your position slightly whilst in the air to be more comfortable.

Carabineers

All carabineers used for short-haul should be of a locking twist or auto-lock design. Both steel and aluminium can be approved. Screw gates are not recommended.

Clothing

Suitable clothing is to be worn by all short haulers; the effects of wind chill, at altitude, over protracted periods of time should not be underestimated.

Knife

A personal emergency knife needs to be carried by every Short Hauler, accessible instantly for emergency use.

Equipment

Large packs, such as medical equipment, SAR Rucksacks can cause additional strain on carabineers and connection devices, as well as severely affect the individuals Centre of Gravity (COG). Equipment is far better placed on its own individual equipment lanyard and kept separate to the Short Hauler.

The part no-one tells you: Release of the recue winch wire, rappel rope or short-haul line is a possible consideration while human external cargo (HEC) is attached beneath the aircraft. This is a difficult discussion to have, but one that needs to be made clearly in training and as part of the on-scene Risk Analysis/ Rescue plan discussion. Every attempt should be made to avoid this situation developing, however, in case of an aircraft emergency, the pilot and rear crew may make the conscious decision to cut the line.

In-flight emergency situations may include:

- Power failure in flight or hover
- Transmission failure
- Tail rotor emergencies
- Full Authority Digital Engine Control (FADEC) failure
- Line or load entanglement
- Turbulence or wind

The decision of any rescuer to cut away from a hoist or line is a personal choice depending on the circumstances and best their chance for survival.

Personnel Safety Check

In all Human external cargo operations, personnel should follow the ´Buddy system´ of equipment checks. This is done as a top to toe check of all PPE:

- Helmet properly fitted; chinstrap fastened.
- Eye protection.
- Fire resistant clothing properly worn.
- No loose items.
- If used - radio operational and on correct frequency.
- Sleeves down and Gloves on.

- Harness properly fitted, buckles correctly fastened, no twists, loose straps secured. Double-check on follow-through buckles.
- Knife easily accessible and secured.
- Approved footwear

Clear and robust communications are paramount; always there will be clear communications between the Short Haulers and the helicopter crew. This can be via radio but is more common using hand signals. To avoid confusion, If short-haulers are inserted in pairs, one person should be responsible for communications and the other for tending to the short-haul rope.

On arrival at the site, the Pilot will conduct a HOGE Power Check, before insertion. Short Haulers will use hand signals to identify direction and altitude adjustments.

Once on the ground enough time will be given to allow correct feet placement and stabilization, before the Short Haulers disconnect. The helicopter may then lower extra medical/ rescue equipment or depart the area to a safe distance, dependent on the plan that has been briefed.

Once the casualty has been recovered, and prior to the helicopter returning for pick up, as part of our CRM practice a useful checklist that can be used for Short Haul Operations and those that utilize a helicopter hoist is the ´SPECTER´ helicopter pre-hoisting check list:

	'SPECTER' - Pre hoist checklist	
S	Stretcher	All buckles/ straps are tight
P	Patient	Do you have? Do you have the correct patient? Is the patient secured correctly into stretcher
E	Environment	Patient and Rescuer Hypothermia protection and PPE
C	Connectors	Buddy check all connectors are correct and securely fastened.
T	Tag-line	If used, is deployed, have ground personnel been briefed on use?
E	Equipment	Is all of your equipment packed, connected, ready to go?
R	Radio/ Ready for pick up	Give ready for pick up signal

The short haul pickup then is a simple reverse of the insertion process. The helicopter will approach, conduct HOGE power checks and deliver the short haul line to you. If you have followed the above checklist, the necessary connectors will be ready in your hand. Simply connect, conduct a physical and visual check that you are connected to the short haul line correctly, the ´Ready for lift´ signal, and the helicopter will extract you from the location.

COMMON ABBREVIATIONS

SAR, HEMS, HAA, TACEVAC, CASEVAC and MEDEVAC?

There are many different terminologies used involving helicopters and aircraft. To better understand what you need, the most common are described:

Air medical services - Is a comprehensive term covering the use of air transportation, airplane or helicopter, to move patients to and from healthcare facilities or accident scenes as required. Personnel provide comprehensive pre-hospital, emergency and critical care to all types of patients during Aeromedical evacuation or rescue operations aboard helicopter and propeller aircraft or jet aircraft.

Search and Rescue (SAR) - The all-weather activity of responding to tasking related to locating and recovering persons in distress, potential distress or missing and delivering them to a place of safety.

HEMS – Helicopter Emergency Medical Service is a flight by a helicopter operating under a HEMS approval, the purpose of which is to facilitate emergency medical assistance, where immediate and rapid treatment and/or transportation is essential, by carrying: (a) medical personnel; (b) medical supplies (equipment, blood, organs, drugs); or (c) ill or injured persons and other persons directly involved.

HAA – Helicopter Air Ambulance, this term replaces the word HEMS in accordance with FAA Circular 135-14B ´Helicopter Air Ambulance Operations´.

MEDEVAC - A military medical evacuation is defined as the timely, efficient movement and enroute care by medical personnel of the wounded, injured, and ill persons, from the battlefield and other locations to treatment facilities. MEDEVAC aircraft, which have medical care providers on board, are mandated by the Geneva Convention to be unarmed and well-marked

CASEVAC/TACEVAC - A Casualty or Tactical Evacuation is the movement of casualties to initial treatment facilities in the combat zone, with potentially no enroute care by medical personnel.

Capabilities and Specifications Definitions

The definitions listed below may clarify the technical specifications of helicopters.

(Remember that these specifications are generally for a "standard day" (altitude = sea level; temperature = 15 degrees C (59 degrees Fahrenheit)).

Parts of a helicopter

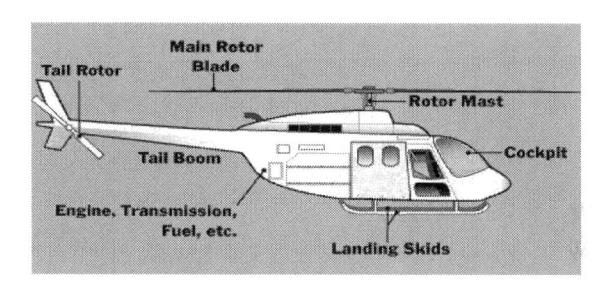

Hover In Ground Effect (HIGE)

HIGE is normally effective up to a height equal to the radius of the main rotor(s). This is measured from the level plane of the main rotor blades to the ground.

Hover Out of Ground Effect (HOGE)

HOGE occurs when the helicopter is hovering out of ground effect.

Gross Weight

"Gross Weight" is the maximum certified weight in pounds. Some models have higher or lower weights for jettisonable external loads.

Useful Load

This number, in pounds, is established by subtracting the average equipped weight of the helicopter from the gross weight.

Fuel Consumption and Fuel Capacity

Fuel consumption, given in pounds per hours, is computed for 5,000 feet pressure altitude at 80 degrees Fahrenheit. Fuel capacity is computed using a measured amount of fuel burned in a known amount of time.

Payload

Pilot and crews use ´tabulated data´ which provides payload data for a variety of temperatures and pressure altitudes. Payload is established by subtracting the equipped weight of the helicopter from the computed Gross Weight on a calm day, at 5,000 feet pressure altitude, 7,400 feet density altitude, 80 degrees Fahrenheit, 2 hours of fuel and crew

Weather and Day / Night Limitations

Weather and Night-time Limitations

Daytime flight operations for most aircraft are limited by Visual Flight Rules (VFR) and they must operate within the following weather minimums;

- One mile (1.6 km) of forward visibility
- 500 ft. (152 m) of clearance below a cloud ceiling
- 1000 ft. (300 m) above clouds
- 2000 ft. (610 m) horizontal clearance from clouds

Additionally, an exception applies to helicopters in "uncontrolled" airspace (Class G) below 1,200 ft. (366 meters) above ground level (AGL); in these areas, helicopters "may be operated clear of clouds if operated at a speed that allows the pilot adequate opportunity to see any air traffic or obstruction in time to avoid a collision" (FAR Part 91.155 b.1).

A helicopter being operating in Class G airspace under FAR PART 135.205 (commercial on demand operations including HEMS) must have 1/2 mile of visibility during the day and one mile of visibility at night. Ultimately, it is best to check with the Helicopter Pilot that you will be working with for any local or State additions, and they may also be able to provide you with invaluable local knowledge to support your own mission goals.

Helicopter Night Rescue Operations

Conducting a night rescue by helicopter in a remote setting dramatically increases operational risk. A study of HEMS accidents found that those air crashes occurring in darkness or bad weather increased the likelihood of a fatal outcome by 95% (FAR Part 1 Baker, Susan, et al. EMS Helicopter Crashes: What Influences Fatal Outcomes?)

It is important to carefully review the option of stabilizing the subject at the scene and initiating the rescue at daybreak.

VFR night flight minimum clearances (the visual distance minimums required for night-time flights) are three statute miles (4.8km) forward visibility and a minimum of 500 ft. (152 m) clearance beneath clouds, furthermore, the FAA permits a helicopter to be operated clear of clouds "at a speed that allows the pilot adequate opportunity to see any air traffic or obstruction in time to avoid a collision." (FAR 91.155(b)(1)). Night Vison Goggles will be covered separately in this manual.

'Land and Live'

A voluntary program designed by the Helicopter international Association (HAI), it is free (you even get a certificate if you take the 'pledge'). What is the pledge?

You will make a precautionary landing if the aircraft has a problem, the pilot feels unwell, anything that may very quickly turn into a real emergency.

I have had the fortune whilst in Guatemala, that all the staff at Helicopteros de Guatemala follow this mantra. It has saved us all many a time. The picture below shows Captain Jorge de Aguila, making a precautionary landing shortly before we approached a mountain range. Moments after this picture, we were 'zero, zero' visibility: a bit of extra patient care was required, but we all lived.

'A Day in the Life' by Mike Boone BSN, RN, CFRN, CCRN

My eyes open to the sound of an alarm filling the black space around me. It is time to work. I quickly orientate myself to the darkness. Here I am, yet again, laying on a foreign, undersized bed. The discomfort all too familiar. I reach for the lamp on the nightstand next to me while simultaneously unplugging my phone from its charger. The pages are already coming across: Coordinates. Ground contact. Patient weight. (If I'm lucky.) I quickly rise, throwing the blankets to an unknown location behind me. My eyes are still adjusting as the rough, Nomex material slides onto my body. My flight suit. *Where are my boots?*

I am halfway zipped, full-leather boots on. My paramedic partner is emerging from the room adjacent to me in a similar, disheveled fashion. We do not even look at each other. Like a coordinated dance, we file down the stairs. Every movement a multi-task as we zip up, grab the blood, grab the narcotics, and enter the hanger. It's go-time. *But what time is it?*

0200, and there she is. Our faithful steed. Patiently waiting to save a life. The pilot completes his flight planning while we, the medical crew, open the hanger door, unplug the helicopter from its wall power, and ready ourselves for the transition outside. While spotting the rotor blades, we receive a second page. The rendezvous location has already changed. We complete our walk-around, flashlights in hand, and enter the aircraft. Our helmets, already donned with NVG's, are placed on our heads. Chip strap secured. It's heavy. I'm reminded that my neck still hurts from the shift before. Our pilot enters the new coordinates into the Garmin navigation system. Tonight, doesn't require a weather check. We're VFR. The night clear as day. The ominous moon shining bright over someone's worse day of their life. Another day in the life for us. Or night, in this case.

Doors closed. Equipment secured. Throttles up. Panel clear. Area clear. We complete our final, pre-flight checklist. *"Dispatch, Rotor One departing with three POB's, 1 hour 45 minutes of fuel, five minutes in route."* 0207. Forcing the wind into submission, we rise from the small dolly. A final hover check, and we're off. We don't contact Tower, because local ATC is closed. But we aren't. We remain silent during sterile cockpit, a critical phase of flight, until we reach cruising altitude. 2000 feet AGL. My partner is already dialing in the frequency for our ground contact while I begin calculating drug dosages on the piece of tape now affixed to my pant leg. Every minute counts. Before I can finish, we arrive.

We circle the veiled landing zone. Law enforcement has attempted to illuminate a 50' by 50' area with small LED's. *I hope they didn't use flairs again.* Hazard. Hazard. Hazard. Too tight. The pilot spots a well-lit parking lot approximately one mile southeast. *"Scene commander, we're going to land at an alternate LZ approximately one mile southeast. It's the high school parking lot. Over."* The location has changed a third time. After another pre-landing brief, we begin our careful descent. Short final. Eyes out. Tower - No factor. Wire - No factor. Light post - No factor. Tail clear. The well-oiled machine is safely on the ground.

We stay hot. Dual engines idled. Rotors turning. *"Off comms."* My partner exits the helicopter and makes his way aft towards the clamshell doors. I am right behind him. The heat expelling from the aircraft's exhaust warms us momentarily while we unload the cot onto the hard surface beneath us. A thumbs up, and we methodically exit the area on the pilot's side at the 2 o'clock position. Just like we practiced. 0215.

A collage of red, white, blue, and yellow surrounds us. Scene is safe. We remove our helmets long enough for patient hand-off. I immediately assign two firefighters in full turnout gear as tail guards. *"Stay close."* I subsequently escort them to the LZ. After a quick head count, the pilot approves our approach with a double flash of the spotlight. The deafening noise of the screaming rotor blades leaves us with gestures as our only means of communication. Hands on, I place the firefighters on their respective sides near the vertical fins. They are the physical barrier between us and the tail rotor of death. This is a deadly business.

My partner finally approaches the helicopter with the patient and two more first responders in the same fashion. After rear-loading the patient, my partner immediately enters the aircraft. After escorting everyone out of the LZ, I perform another walk-around and follow suit. Another pre-flight check, another challenge and response, and we pull pitch. Our patiently lays helplessly on the cot, but we are eyes out. Priorities of survival. Out of the LZ, but not out of harm's way, we ascend to cruising altitude. It is time to work. Maintain situational awareness. *Do your job.* My partner turns on the dim cabin light for a source of illumination as I begin to work.

0228. 10-minute ETE. We call report to the receiving facility. *"What's the patient's name again?"* Silence takes us once more. We have done this before. Our coordinated dance continues as equipment and supplies are exchanged between my partner and me. We already know what needs to happen. The muffled hum of the rotor blades set the tempo for our urgent pace. 30 minutes of work needs to happen in 10 minutes. *Work slower. Work smoother. Work faster.* I internalize the mantra until we arrive. A rush to the ED, a safe hand-off, it's over. The patient is alive. For now.

We are back at base. 0320. Mission completed. Mission successful? The PIC initiates the post-transport debrief process. He opens the floor for the medical crew's input. *"What could we have done better?"*

- Make sure your boots are nearby and accessible, so that our departure is not delayed.
- ATC was closed for the night. Make sure you report our position to area traffic when applicable.
- The landing area changed three times. Perform outreach education on appropriate LZ specifications ASAP.
- Consider minimizing the amount of non-flight crew members brought under the rotor blades.
- Consider minimizing cabin lights to avoid reducing night vision. Lip lights are an approved source of illumination.

As we wrap up, the tones drop a second time. 0340. We look at each other with a slight grin. It is time to do it all over again.

CREW RESOURCE MANAGEMENT

When to Use a Helicopter

Helicopters may be utilized to efficiently extricate a subject from an otherwise inaccessible accident scene. Situations that involve remote locations with critical injuries are very appropriate for a helicopter-based rescue.

An injured subject can then be transferred to a helicopter emergency medical service (HEMS) aircraft or ground based ambulance, as appropriate, with the proper continuity of care being provided.

When multiple transportation options are available, rescuers should determine which technique offers the least risk and greatest gain both for rescuers and the casualty. Evaluate the totality of the circumstances surrounding the incident, including the duration and difficulty of a conventional evacuation, rescuer and patient safety, the severity of the patient's injury, current and projected environmental hazards, personnel and aircraft availability, and transport time to a definitive care facility. The following questions can assist in the decision to use a helicopter for rescue:

- Are conditions adequate for communication with all involved rescue personnel, or do communications barriers exist?
- Is a safe landing site available within a reasonable distance of the accident site?
- Does the urgency of the subject's condition require getting someone to the accident site as quickly as possible?
- Is the risk associated with traversing terrain to the accident scene greater than the risk of using specialized helicopter rappel, short-haul, or hoisting techniques?
- Are all helicopter crewmembers proficient with the helicopter rescue technique being considered?
- Does altitude or environmental factors prevent the use of a helicopter?
- Would the immediate insertion of advanced life support (ALS) care direct to the scene downgrade an urgent medical case to a lower priority ground evacuation?
  - Insertion of a trained EMS provider, who conducts a proper assessment, may permit appropriately downgrading the rescue plan to a ground ambulance transport of the patient.

Ultimately, the decision to use a helicopter falls into two categories:

1. **According to the patient's condition (the severity of illness or injury),**
2. **According to the circumstances at the site of the incident.**

The old concept of helicopter emergency Medevac (first used extensively in Korea in support of MASH hospitals, that ultimately came of age in the Vietnam war), was where a wounded soldier could be in a forward surgical unit within 30 minutes after receiving a pickup by Medical Helicopter. Since then as the civilian Helicopter Emergency Medical / Rescue operations have developed the approach has now changed. Utilizing Pre-hospital lessons learnt in the war in

Afghanistan and through various services around the world, the aim is no longer to achieve a ´fast pick-up´ and get the patient to Definitive Medical care within the Golden hour. The role of helicopters today is to take advanced lifesaving care to the patient, so the traditional ´Golden Hour' has been altered:

- Vital intervention must be received within the first ten minutes, known as the Platinum Ten;
- Emergency first aid and lifesaving interventions within an hour,
- The first definitive surgery must be carried out by the two-hour mark

Outside of an active combat environment, adopting this framework, if the equipment is available, allows a crew to reduce risk, by not ´rushing´ on scene as a crew has more time to conduct interventions to stabilize the patient before flight if necessary.

Crew Resource Management

Flight crew actions or "human factors" are the primary factor in nearly all aviation accidents. Of the total of a fatalities,

- 68 % accidents involve Human Error
- 30 % involve weather
- 25 % from mechanical fault
- 20 % controlled flight into terrain (CFIT)

Of all of these, the majority are all preventable.

These statistics directly lead to the development of a training program known as Cockpit Resource Management (CRM) or "crew resource management" as the concept began to involve personnel outside of the flight deck. CRM is also useful outside the aviation industry and has been found to be highly effective for improving team performance in any high-risk environment. CRM directly addresses the errors caused by poor group decision making, ineffective communication, inadequate leadership, and poor task or resource management.

A team employing effective CRM utilizes open communications, briefings, team member advocacy, crew monitoring, crosschecking, task vigilance, effective workload management, improved situational awareness, fatigue and distraction avoidance, and promotes an environment of self-critique and a recent focus as per military operations is the increased (and correct use) of checklists.

Good CRM relies on the dedicated actions of people, which are unfortunately not without flaws. A breakdown in effective CRM repeatedly leads to accidents. During helicopter rescue operations, effective CRM needs be achieved not only amongst the flight crew but also extend outside of the aircraft to include communications personnel (dispatch), ground rescuers, incident command staff, and any additional responding agencies.

One of the best means to practice good CRM is through effective and professional communication strategies, which eliminate confusion and avoid assuming information has been adequately shared. The importance of several of the communications strategies and techniques found within this survival book i.e. conducting briefings, checklists and utilizing direct statements all contribute to improved CRM.

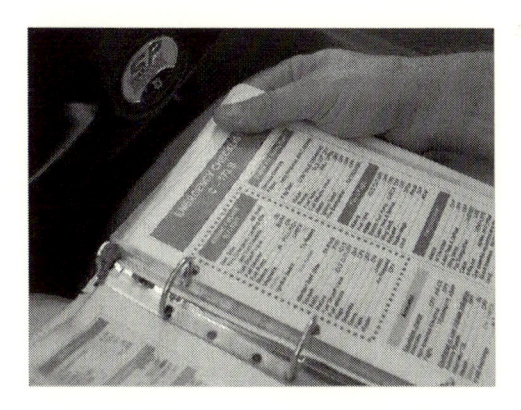

Before moving into how CRM plays a critical role in HEMS, one must first understand the foundations of CRM and the concepts that may be applied to any team that means to mitigate risk of error in high acuity procedures and situations.

"Amateurs practice until they get it right. Experts practice until they cannot get it wrong.'-
Graham Chalk

Human Factors:

The multidisciplinary field of human factors research is devoted to optimizing human performance and reducing human error. It is the applied science that studies people working together with machines. Individuals who study human factors recognize and bring to light inadequate system design, product design, or operator training that can contribute to an individual human error or series of errors by multiple individuals that leads to a catastrophic failure.

Crew Resource Management (CRM):

CRM is the application of team management concepts in a high-risk environment. Team management typically recognizes the use of techniques, procedures, and tools for a group to achieve a common goal. The key difference is that CRM applies concepts from team management to tasks in which errors have significant ramifications. Moreover, it is the efficient and effective use of all available resources: human, hardware, and information. This paper defines the scope of CRM to include all human elements involved in coordination, decision-making, and purpose of the flight. It includes all pieces of equipment (helmets, fire suits), materials (written checklists), concepts (dual decision making, cross checking), behaviours, attitudes, and skills that may be employed in safe practices.

Crew Monitoring (CM):

Crew monitoring is a method of error prevention that is an integral part of CRM. It is visual verification that a task is properly executed by another member of the flight crew. An example of CM may be a medical crewmember sitting in the cockpit verifying that the pilot is about to toggle the correct switch. Monitoring is an essential skill in HEMS as the medical crew (non-aviation) can aid the pilot considerably in avoiding a CFIT accident by scanning the flight path periodically. Cross-Checking, which is similar to the concept of crew monitoring, may be more verbal and formalized whereas CM may be performed without the monitored member of the team being aware of the event.

Decision-making and Conflict Resolution:

When working as a team no decision is to be made alone. Dual decision-making is always an available resource which allows the pilot and any other member of the flight team to confer on a decision before action is taken. If there is a disagreement in the correct course of action, proper attitudes and behaviours will ensure that the conflict is resolved while maintaining the integrity of the flight.

Upper Management Commitment:

CRM should be applied through an organization in a top down method. If upper management supports and reinforces CRM concepts, they are much more likely to disseminate to employees in operations

Components of a CRM Program

Successful implementation of CRM requires the utilization of several concepts that are published with regularity in text:

Standard Operating Procedures (SOP's): Standard Operating Procedures (SOPs): SOPs are the strategic architecture around which operations are to be carried out including CRM. Desired components of CRM would be clearly defined in the SOPs which crewmembers would be trained to follow. The SOPs of a HEMS organization would incorporate policies such as sterile cockpit policy, usage of pilot-crew challenge and response, and the integration of equipment such as TAWS. SOPs should reflect the shared mental model upon which good crew performance depends.

Initial and recurrent training: Studies show that initial CRM training is extremely effective however the desirable behaviours taught by CRM extinguish or disappear without regular recurrent training.

Briefings: Daily, Pre- and post-flight (debrief) briefings are a critical component to CRM, as they involve all members of the team in information verification and reinforce a safety culture.

Closed Loop Communication: Closed loop communication so that miscommunications are a rare event. (Closed loop communication involves the confirmation that information was understood correctly by repeating the statement just heard.)

Reinforcement: Immediate closed loop feedback as to a task which has been completed

Maintaining Situational Awareness: A constant review of the flight and systems status by the operator, which is vigilantly crosschecked by the other members of the flight team.

Workload Management: Recognition by the Pilot in Command (PIC) that the demands of flight are reaching or have reached a critical point and subsequently the proper delegation of tasks to available crewmembers

Recommendations for HEMS programs

Develop a customized and comprehensive CRM-based Safety Culture:

Review the recommendations from the Federal Aviation Administration Crew Resource Management Training Advisory Circular AC 120-51E for further in-depth guidance.

Crews should strive to incorporate the many concepts of CRM into its safety organization and daily operating procedures. The more CRM is a part of an organization the more its concepts and practices disseminate into the behaviours of its individuals. The effectiveness of a safety culture starts with the first day of employment.

Developing a strong foundation of SOP's that incorporate all of the practices.

Have specific policies and procedures for all aspects of the aeromedical and helicopter rescue role pertinent to our area of operations. The more specific and comprehensive they become, the more specific individual and crew behaviours will become.

Train on a Daily Basis

Daily training does not require high fidelity simulation with sophisticated equipment. Practices such as 'chair flying' can be equally effective when practiced correctly. Have mandated training allocated during your daily working routine.

Pre-and Post-Flight Briefings

Crews will hold formalized briefings and debriefings in accordance with Policy Documents

Challenge and Response Checklists

Incorporation C&R Checklists into Pre-take off and pre-landing procedures. These 'Challenge-verification-response' checklists are extremely effective at identifying errors and verifying tasks have been correctly executed.

Abolish response times which place undue pressure on Pilots

Crews will not launch prior to pre-take off procedures being correctly completed.

ICS Isolation of cockpit from cabin

Crews are not to isolate the ICS system at any time. Correct 'Sterile Cockpit' procedures are to be adopted.

'Sterile Cockpit' - *In 1981, the U.S. Federal Aviation Administration (FAA) enacted Federal Aviation Regulations (FARS) Part 171.542 for air carriers and Part 135.100 for air taxi operators. "Flight Crew Member Duties", also known in the industry as the "sterile cockpit rule", are the subject of these two parts of the FARS. These regulations prohibit crew members from performing non-essential duties or activities while the aircraft is in a "critical phase of flight"*. *The FARs define "critical phase of flight" as all ground operations involving taxing, take-off and landing and all other flight operations conducted below 10,000 feet (3050 meters) mean sea level (MSL), except cruise flight.*

Incorporate a formalized written risk assessment into every mission.

Utilise the 'GAR Risk Assessment prior to accepting any mission. Dynamic Risk Assessments are conducted throughout all stages of the operation.'

Communications

Communication is everything on a HELICOPTER operation. Without "good communications," safety is quickly jeopardized as personnel accountability is lost and responders begin free-lancing without specific direction. Clear precise communications eliminate the pitfalls that have jeopardized many missions.

Common hand signals are covered during the practical phase of the Helicopter Essentials course, and are useful when combined with radio transmissions, because they are instantly understood and avoid the problems of garbled messages and radio frequency congestion.

There a many different signals to indicate everything an aircraft needs, and they can be different from fixed to rotor wing and will vary slightly dependent on Country.

However, in many cases pilots and are crews who are not familiar with or confident of the ground personnel using the hand signals and/ or may ignore the signals or rely on their own best judgment instead.

Working and training in advance builds the necessary trust and familiarity between aircrews and ground rescuers. Emergency responders must have reliable communication equipment and possess effective personal communication skills.

Using Direct Statements

As stated previously, the sharing of critical information provides an accurate mental model for personnel.

Flight crews adhere to a "sterile cockpit," refraining from non-essential or extraneous conversation, during critical phases of flight (e.g. landing, take-off, hover, hoist operations, etc.).

All personnel should be taught to violate this mandate if they have urgent safety-related communication required for the safe operation of the aircraft. There is no room for ´Ego´ or unwillingness to speak to a superior member of the team. If there is a problem or potentially dangerous situation developing it needs to be addressed immediately.

Emergency responders often observe operational hazards during an incident; however, they fail to speak up to initiate getting them corrected. In situations involving critical communication, it is most effective to use direct statements. Although they appear rude, direct statements are difficult to ignore and are very productive.

The following are the six components of direct statements:

1. Address the person to whom you are talking by name.
2. Begin with, "I," "I think," "I believe," or "I feel."
3. State your message or solution as clearly as possible.
4. Use the appropriate emotion for your message so that it's delivered as you intended.
5. Require a response by using such statements as "What do you think?" or "Don't you agree?"
6. Don't let the matter go. Don't disengage with the other person until you achieve agreement or buy-in.

An example of a direct statement might be, "Pilot, I think that aircraft approaching us on the left at 9 o´clock looks dangerous. What do you think?

It may sound simple, but this technique is very effective. A direct statement gets the person's attention and forces the individual to deal with your concern rather than allowing him or her to ignore your message.

Preplanning and Mission Planning

For a helicopter rescue operation to succeed, enough preplanning must be done well in advance of the initial notification. Helicopter crews will conduct most of this planning themselves with no external input, however for better professional standards and inter-operability Rescue teams should develop an in-depth knowledge of and working rapport with aviation resources through meetings and advanced training.

For those personnel unfamiliar with the flight Briefing process, dependent on the mission parameters, helicopter provider and professionalism they will usually involve a number of personnel, from the crew selected to fly the mission, Chief Pilots and Safety Staff, Operational Managers and Maintenance Staff all who will give Professional input to ensure any mission is conducted safely.

Most briefings also rely on extensive use of Operational and Procedures manuals in order to make sure that no mistakes are made.

A briefing should take no longer than a maximum of 15 minutes, if a complex operation pre prepare the following information and display it (as it's the main thing people want to know in all honesty):

1. What time do we start?
2. What time do we finish?
3. What is my job?
4. Who am I working with?

If the intention is to use or work closely with a Helicopter Rescue Team, the following Mission Planning process is a simple process to brief, allowing the most important information to be acted on accordingly:

Mission Plan – T.S.M.E.A.C. S

T	**Topography**	Description of the terrain, geography & environment the mission is being conducted in
S	**Situation**	Statement of what the current situation is
M	**Mission**	Clear explanation of the goal
E	**Execution**	Step by step list of how the mission is going to be performed
A	**Administration & Logistics**	Description of equipment/gear to be used, job delegations & contingency plans
C	**Command & Signals**	Chain of Command, communication methods and timings
S	**Safety**	Identified hazards & specific requirements

As part of the pre-planning process, it is also worth considering preparing in advance the following information:

- Type of Medical / Rescue equipment carried – each weighed separately.

- Your Medical / Rescue Teams individual weights.

- You may also consider preparing an aerial hazard map for the area that identifies wires, power lines, in addition to established Helicopter landing sites and staging areas (for example open parks, football pitches, tourist spots) with known coordinates.

Pre-planning aids dramatically in times of Rescue, key information is already briefed and 90% of preparation is done.

Aircraft Weight and Balance

It is vital to comply with the weight and balance limits established for each individual helicopter. Operating above the maximum weight limitation compromises the structural integrity of the helicopter and adversely affects performance. Balance is also critical because on some fully loaded helicopters, center of gravity (CG) deviations by a few inches can dramatically change a helicopter's handling characteristics.

In fixed-wing aircraft, the load is balanced over a horizontal wing area and has a comparatively wide range. In a helicopter, however, it is carried under a single point, the rotor mast. Therefore, even a small amount of loading discrepancy can greatly affect the pilot's ability to control the helicopter.

To ensure that a helicopter is not exceeding maximum gross weight (equipped weight plus entire load), a load calculation should be prepared before any mission which is completed by the pilot. This might be viewed as an unnecessary delay during an emergency operation; however, the completion of an accurate load calculation is an essential flight planning tool.

Pre-weighing equipment and clearly marking this weight on the outside of the bags, streamlines payload calculations for the aircrew during an operational response. To determine whether a helicopter is within the weight limits, you must consider the weight of the basic helicopter, crew, passengers, cargo, and fuel.

Equipment may be in modules for specific tasks i.e. Module A – Cliff Rescue, Module B – BLS Equipment to save time and the chance of forgetting an essential piece of gear.

If operating separately / away from the helicopter base this information can then be passed to aircrew i.e. ´Require Modules A and D...'

Checklists

As part of good CRM, Even the most experienced Rescue Crewman still follow a checklist, one for the helicopter and then one separate for the evolution being undertaken.

Whether situated on a kneeboard, or wrist panel, don't create a checklist for your checklist. They should contain the bullet points only, and any CRM words of Command.

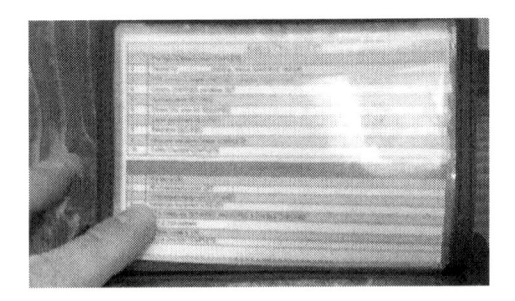

Checklists are used in a verbal 'Challenge and Response' format, irrespective of operator experience.

Post Mission

Following every helicopter operation there should be a ´Hot De-brief´. These have been proven as a main ´key´ ingredient of all successful teams. A culture of ´No blame/ No ego´ should be actively encouraged and is designed to

- Provide feedback to involved personnel.
- Identify areas of concern for follow up.
- Reinforce lesson learned.

A simple approach is to review each of the headings you briefed using the ´TSMEACS´ format. Did you achieve your mission? Lessons learnt/ mistakes? Equipment deficiencies?

The aim is to make us safer and better – ALL OF THE TIME…

The key to effective utilization of any resource in helicopter operation lies in the following factors:

- Early identification of the requirements
- Effective mobilization of the required resources
- Efficient management of the resources at the scene
- Accountability for resource utilization

With helicopter resource management, additional concerns are vital to the success of the operation. These are:

- Assurance that safety considerations are not only met, but exceeded
- A complete risk-benefit analysis is performed prior to the utilization of any aircraft

With proper management of airborne resources, search and rescue teams can accomplish more than is possible with simply ground-based resources.

Once again, "helicopter management" is "the direction, scheduling, coordination and control of helicopter use in accordance with agency policies to ensure maximum efficiency as well as safety in all aspects of the search or rescue operation."

When it goes wrong...

A very sad and common experience is crews being put at risk, whether through 'helicopter shopping, reverse helicopter shopping' or whichever terminology is the flavor of the month. So even if you a robust and proven safety system in place, a flight safety committee, all the strategies that we should have in place: and you are still conducting dangerous missions. Whether through lack of training, administrative/ financial burden, whatever external pressure.

To put into context, you have done a flight, your company had 'adjusted the weather minimums', it has been refused by another company potentially. Due to whatever reason you fly, end up IIMC and is not a pleasant experience for all onboard the helicopter.

WHAT DO YOU DO?

Inform your flight safety committee, if operating with SMS in place, the report goes directly to the CEO. What else.

IT IS VERY SIMPLE.

You report the Pilot in Command (PIC) to their relevant Aviation Authority. Simple.

Is it that simple? Well it is, I expect 100 percent to be reported if I get it wrong and break the law.

So does the Pilot.

a) It's part of the job, and
b) The Pilot remember has ultimate authority and responsibility for that aircraft in accordance with the law. If he breaks the law. Report it.

Would you report a drunk driver to the Police, who nearly hit a group of school kids?

Would you report a medic who overdosed a patient?

This is a Professional career we do – treat it as such.

Aviation Law is there for a reason, minimums are legally defined for a reason. Break them – is only one person's fault. All the safety systems, risk assessments and procedures we have in place, the support we give the Pilot as a qualified crewmember are all there to support one person in making the final decision.

The Pilot.

The Pilot is the pinnacle of the triangle, everything else we do is there to support and assist them in doing their job.

'A Day in the Life' by Jordan White BSN, RN, CFRN, ACNP-S

The alarm clock begins to screech as I roll over and silence it out of routine. I slip out of the covers and walk down the stairs to by bags packed by the door, ready for the shift ahead. I toss the bags into the truck and begin the four-hour journey to work. The company I work for is unique due to their schedule. Full time is nine shifts a month, twenty-four-hour shifts. Due to our strict fatigue management system, we are allowed to work up to six days in a row. Few companies in the states provide this schedule to their crews. As I kiss my wife goodbye, I know that it will be 4-6 days before I see her again. My morning routine is simple, I use my drive for education and rejuvenation. My education is typically catching up on my favorite medical or HEMS related podcast and my rejuvenation is my cup of coffee. When I arrive to work, I meet the "off going" crew. We chat, share some breakfast or coffee and discuss their previous shift. Any pertinent information is relayed to the oncoming crew such as aircraft issues, supplies or base needs. We check in with the comm (communication) center and are officially on duty. The on-duty pilot then briefs us for the day. This is usually updating us on any weather moving in, aircraft maintenance that is coming due as well as any plans for the day such as outreach. Once the morning briefs are done, we normally head out to the aircraft to inspect it as well as our medical equipment. We all trust our crews, but my motto is "trust but verify." If something is missing or not working, it is your responsibility to find it. After this, I like to knock out education or work requirements. This could range from completing a newly assigned online module, updating my certifications or performing the mandatory training requirements set forth by the company as well as CAMTS. After this, the job is what most drool over. The rest of the day is yours. From video games, movies and even workouts, you are able to choose how you spend your day. Getting in naps is not only a good idea but is strongly encouraged by the company so that you are well rested for the night. TONES DROP. This is what the job is known for right? The cell phone lights up with the text page. It reads something like this: LAUNCH Interfacility (IFT) request. 59 Female. 97KG. If we are not "green" for weather, we discuss the condition with the pilot, and all view the radar and forecast. At this point, once all three crew members reply ACCEPT, we receive patient information via text. We stop whatever we are doing, suit up and head to the awaiting aircraft. If our pilot is there first, he is typically spinning up prior to our arrival. We do our modified 360 walk-round (blades are turning). This means we walk from the end of one skid, around to the next skid and visually inspect the tail. We are looking for any debris or objects on the pad. We are scanning the aircraft for loose latches or any fluids leaking onto the concrete below. We are checking that seat belts are not stuck in the doors. This is an extremely important safety inspection that can easily become habitual. Eventually, crews begin to see what they have always seen. Make a conscious effort to be engaged in all aspects of safety. Safety and communication are paramount in this career. As a new flight member or veteran, becoming and maintaining an attitude of safety is imperative. From there, we are belted in and ready for departure. All of what you have just read happens in under 10 minutes. During flight we work as a cohesive team. Every move is carefully calculated and weighed. When lifting from the pad, as we do daily, the pilot will still call out, "tail coming right." Whoever is sitting on the right side will look out and call "tail clear." You are not just a flight clinician; you are a member of the team. Communicate, your life depends on it. We arrive to the bedside for the IFT or the scene and begin care. The patient is transported to the accepting facility or the closest depending on the call. Handoff is performed to the accepting MD or RN and care is transferred. One of the most important aspects of the flight, per any flight crew member, would be the snack room at the destination. Food is never promised! Eat when you can! After we have a few snacks, its back up to the helipad to head home. At this point, the call is usually halfway done. The flight home can be used to knock some charting out but typically the chart is done back at base. An easy flight may require an hour of charting whereas a more complex flight could take 2-3 hours to chart. Typically, whoever isn't charting is in charge of restocking supplies we used. Once the chart is done, and the supplies restocked, we go back to our cold food, or unpause the movie! When people ask what it's like to be a flight nurse, I usually use the cheesy pun, "it has its ups and downs." In reality, its much like a fire department. The family feel, the camaraderie and the ebbs and flows of calls give it that feel. Some shifts it may be boring and drag by when flights are infrequent. Other days, it takes all you have to simply find time to use the restroom. The best days tend to be in the middle. Periods of boredom followed by brief moments of shear adrenaline. What most flight crews do not discuss, due to lack of sparkle and Hollywood, are the calls that may not be exhilarating or exciting. The 0300hrs call for a stable septic patient, or the patient who missed dialysis and now needs emergency dialysis. Others do not see the hours of intense, continuous training that goes into the job. Flight is an amazing career that gives many people the autonomy and adrenaline they crave. As with any public safety position, it comes often without the glimmer and shine; without the appreciation for what you do. If you love to fly, care for the extremely sick and the not so sick patient, and feel that you make a difference, flying is for you. My advice to anyone starting out in this industry would be this...while at work you are first a mother, a father or spouse.... you are a flight clinician secondly. Having safety first and foremost will help ensure you come home to them.

SURVIVAL

Before accumulating information on the use and operation of survival equipment, it is important to first understand the psychological barriers to the will to survive that must be overcome. The most predominant psychological barrier to survival is fear: fear of the unknown, fear of discomfort, and fear of one's own weakness. Fear of the environment leads us to fear our own chances of survival, and even though we overcome these fears to some extent, a lack of confidence in our ability may weaken our will to survive.

Studies of survivors and their experiences show that the successful survival of any situation depends on several factors. The survivor must:

- Be mentally and spiritually prepared for the possibility of long-term survival;

- Be in good physical condition;

- Have the tools and equipment available and know how to use it;

- Be properly dressed for any survival situation;

- Be thoroughly familiar with emergency egress procedures.

The key to these experiences is developing a survivor's "attitude". In other words, to develop those traits and characteristics that will enhance one's chance of survival

The Will to Survive

There are several factors that will influence a crew member's ability to survive in the event the aircraft is forced to make an emergency landing or crash in a remote area. These are mental characteristics that each crew member should strive to maintain while dealing with a potentially stressful situation.

Having the physical skills to survive the event will do little good if the right outlook and attitude are not present.

Courage: Enables us to overcome the fear that can overwhelm us in a survival situation. Each time we encounter danger or fear and overcome it, we strengthen our courage. It is understandable that crew members will exhibit a certain amount of fear in these situations the key is to not allow that fear to become panic.

Determination: is a state of mind in which you tell yourself that you will overcome whatever obstacle you are faced with.

Survival Cheerfulness: The ability to maintain a cheerful and humorous attitude despite being placed in a stressful situation will allow crew members to overcome many of the anxieties and the apprehension they face.

Positive Attitude: Being positive helps make the best out of the current situation. Thoughts of failure will hinder the ability to make sound and clear decisions. Failure is inevitable when one believes there is no hope in sight.

Purpose: Having a sense of purpose and setting goals (both long and short term) will help keep crew members motivated. Being motivated is has a high value in a survival situation because it assists in generating the will to live.

Productiveness: Keeping busy will increase crew member's chances for survival by keeping both the mind and body occupied.

Certainty: The will to survive is inevitably dependent on the crew's ability to remain certain that they will once again return to family, friends and co-workers. You are only a survivor once you have returned to civilization.

Priorities of Survival

In most of the world, extensive Search and Rescue Organizations exist. Developing countries may have nothing available at all, and the local assets available should be part of your Pre-mission planning and preparation.

However, the possibility still exists that a person may be forced to spend 24-72 hours in a remote area while a SAR operation is organized and implemented or bad weather clears. Knowing what steps are most important will help establish goals and provide you with a framework for which to operate under.

Over many years, the ´Priorities of Survival´ have been developed. These are derived from what is known as the "Rule of Threes";

- 3 seconds following a bad decision,
- 3 minutes without oxygen,
- 3 Hours exposed to extreme cold,
- 3 days without water,
- 3 weeks without food

Because of these rules, the priorities of survival can be established that focus on the most important actions:

1. **PROTECTION** - Protection from the elements, weather, insects and further injury are all covered in this section.

2. **LOCATION** – We want to be FOUND and be RESCUED
3. **WATER** – Collection and preservation of water
4. **FOOD** – Not an immediate priority, but necessary to prevent hypoglycemia and malnutrition

These guidelines however do not consider the most important action in any aircraft survival situation and that is to first, evacuate from a damaged aircraft using emergency egress procedures. Once evacuation is complete and crews have performed a medical first aid, they can turn their attention to the priorities of survival.

´Dress to Egress´

So, what is the term ´Dress to Egress´? It is part of the priority of survival ´Protection´ and it is simply to wear the correct clothing required (and need) to have on you in the event of a crash landing. The key terminology here is ´wear´, if you are cold walking to your aircraft, then you are dressed incorrectly.

There is however a balance between dressing correctly and over dressing so that you cannot accomplish your actual job.

Helmets:

In HEMS or SAR work, you simply have to wear a helmet. Unlike commercial passenger carrying helicopters, we do not have to keep the client pleased with how we look (i.e. why do they wear helmets and we don't). **Blunt Trauma is the leading cause of death in helicopter accidents**.

So why not wear one? There are many different options available and they range from simple conversion kits for standard aviation headsets (such as the David Clark Model pictured) to factory manufactured purpose-built helicopter helmets.

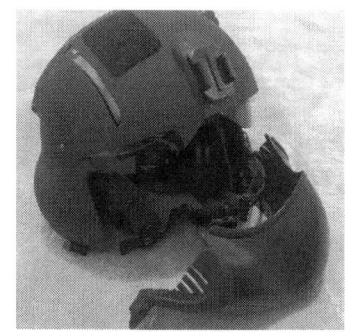

CEP, ANR, lenses color? All are extras dependent on personal choice – it's the actual helmet that will (potentially) save you. One addition commonplace now is the addition of a Maxillofacial Screen, designed to provide lower face protection, whilst reducing wind noise.

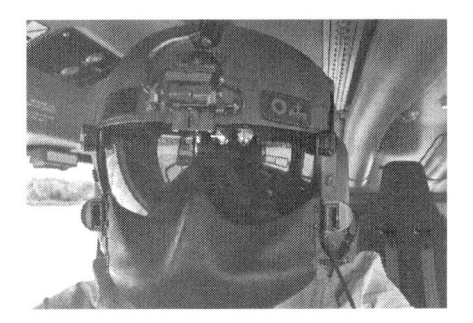

3M ® reflective tape

A cross of reflective tape is useful for several reasons, if doing Human External Cargo operations, the helicopter crew can see you better, if in the water during a survival event, its highly visible for those looking for you!

Helicopter ICS Jack Plug ports are normally at a 90-degree angle to the direction you exit. If you forget to unplug your ICS cord, you will get approximately both feet on the ground outside the aircraft, before your head and neck are yanked backwards. This has killed people in emergencies, as the time it takes to disconnect, the emergency has worsened.

A simple way to overcome this (for all flight crew) is to use a communications extension lead (wandering lead).

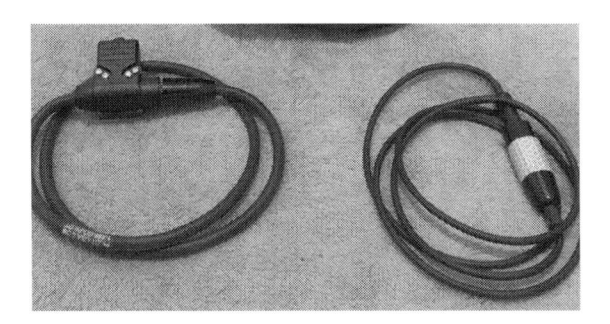

There are generally two types of wandering lead. The one on the left includes a Press to Talk Switch (PTT), that overrides the voice activation system (VOX) of the helicopter so that you can only speak when you 'press to talk' as opposed to 'Hot Mike'. The other type on the right is a simple extension lead and both types allow more freedom of movement in and around the aircraft, as they are available in a multitude of lengths.

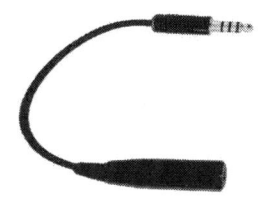

The non-PTT type are now being made available especially in an approximately 30 cm length, specifically to alleviate the emergency egress problem as a result of lessons learnt. Irrespective of length, if you forget to disconnect as you are egressing in an emergency, as the cables become horizontal, the male/ female jack plugs simply disconnect.

Microphones

Depending on your helmet manufacturer, there are a multitude of different microphones available. The first important thing to note however, is that are there are two distinct differences:

1. HIGH Impedance – Civilian helicopters
2. LOW Impedance – Military helicopters

Get the wrong one, in the wrong helicopter and it wont work. Either swap out the microphone for the one you need, or if you regularly switch aircraft types, a converter can be bought that runs on a 9v battery.

One key piece of equipment is a foam covering, this eliminates a lot of ambient noise, they occasionally fall off (which is annoying!), so use a small cable/ 'zip tie':

Helmet Bags

Keeps your helmet protected, and allows you to carry spares, extra gloves and snack bars!

I have the extra large 'Jumbo' version, as it accommodates a helmet with a Maxiofacial screen better. The picture shows the size comparison between a 'regular/ standard' size and a 'Jumbo'. The red 'Remove before flight' streamer, is not for fashion, is because everyone looks to see what it is and you don't forget your gear!

What do I keep in it?

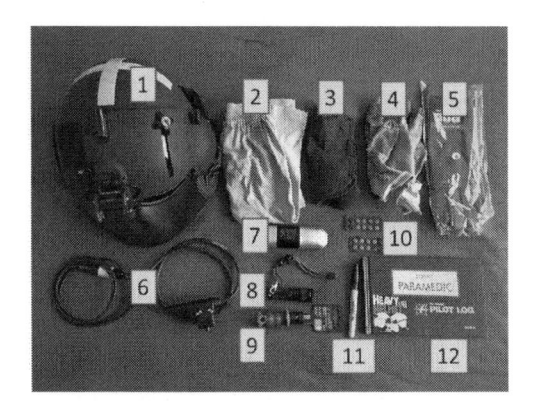

1. Helmet (when not wearing obviously!)
2. Nomex ® neck 'buff'
3. Skull cap
4. Hoist gloves

5. Nomex ® touch screen gloves (new!)
6. 2x wandering leads: PTT and normal
7. Visor cleaning kit
8. Spare torch
9. Short flat head screwdriver (to tighten helmet screws when needed)
10. Anti-emetic (motion sickness) tablets
11. Spare Sharpie pen
12. Flight hours logbook

Flight Gloves

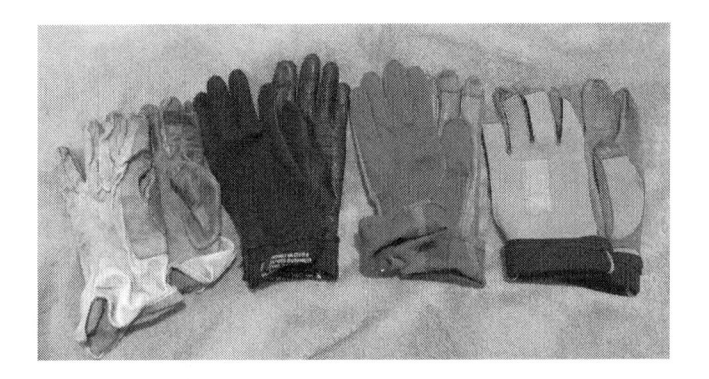

Pictured Left to Right: UK SAR Winch Operator, USA Black Nomex, USA Nomex touchscreen, UK SAR Winchman neoprene gloves/

Why wear gloves? Apart from the obvious to keep your hands warm, or absorb sweat in hot climates – they are primarily for your protection against:

- Fire – Many aircrews have successfully escaped the aircraft only to be engulfed in the Flash Fire that follows
- Injury protection against poorly fitted cockpits / flight deck fixtures, fittings and screws

- And they help in finger retention for those who persist in wearing rings in the workplace....

Dependent on country of origin, the most common are the US style Nomex and kid leather variants with British flight gloves tending to be all kid leather.

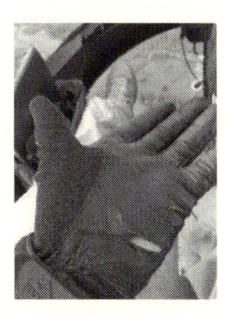

Gloves with holes (as in the picture of my hand) or with finger ends cut of (to provide better dexterity), obviously provide less protection and need to be replaced or repaired. So, keep a spare pair in your helmet/ flight bag, so if you damage during flight operations you can immediately replace and retain protection for your hands.

For those that utilize touch screen devices, available on the commercial market are 'touch screen compatible' Nomex ® gloves. Like with everything, there are good designs, and some uncomfortable ones, try before you buy!

Flight suits

These came to the fore during World War 1, and various types of one and two-piece outfits were developed among pilots to ward off the chill caused by propwash and the cold of low-oxygen high-altitude flying.

Leather quickly became the preferred material due to its durability and the protection against oil thrown off by the simple rotary and inline motors of the time.

In 1917 Australian aviator Frederick Sidney Cotton's developed the revolutionary "Sidcot" suit, this flying suit, with improvements, was widely used by the British RAF until the 1950s.

The world-famous World War 1 fighter ace ´Baron von Richtofen (The Red Baron) ´ was wearing a confiscated Sidcot suit when he was shot down.

One piece or Two piece? Thick or thin?

Most individuals and companies tend to utilize the flight suits based on United States military design, as they are mass produced in varying colors and easy to obtain. What many people aren't aware that the military options are usually available in two different thicknesses: Summer weight and winter weight (For example: CWU 27/P or CWU 64/P), so if you are constantly too hot (or too cold!), check what type you have.

Sleeves need to rolled down fully, to prevent the exposure of skin at the top of your gloves, and a little known fact is that the ´collar´ is actually designed to be worn up (think ´Elvis´) – to provide fire protection to the nape of your neck.

Many providers now offer flight suits in two pieces, these have the benefit of you being able to remove the top half if stranded unexpectedly overnight somewhere (so you don't have to walk round looking like Top Gun all night), and are obviously easier for ´calls of nature´. I have never been a fan of two piece as you tend to get a gap appear in the waist region when bent over (and can get very cold!), however I am recently trialing a customized pair of 'Rotor wash' pants from StephanH flight clothing in Canada. They are a light weight Nomex ® material, with removable kneepads, and pockets that I have asked to be included. They are proving very beneficial whilst instructing, and for routine flights where not doing hoist ops and underslung cargo type work (where the rear crew end up hanging out of the side doors at all kinds of strange angles).

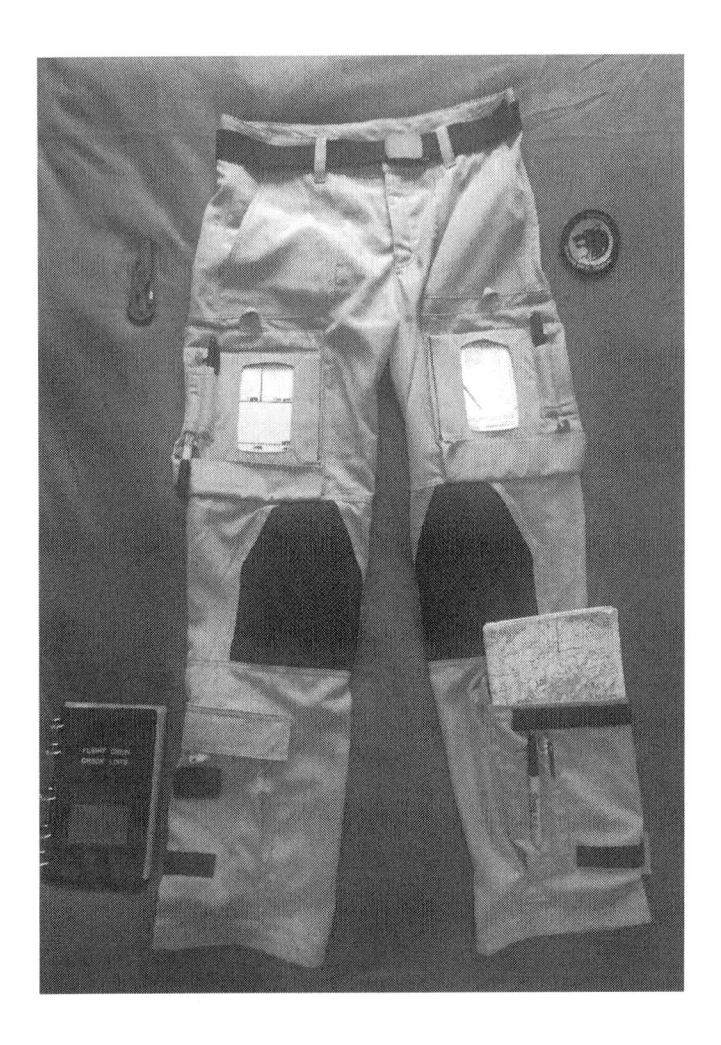

Fire protection.

Certain countries have regulations/ legislation that 'recommend' a fire-resistant material. For example our Standard Operating Procedures (SOPs) do not mandate FR clothing for certain operations, for two reasons, primarily as normally the material is too thick and hot and our risk matrices determine heat stroke a higher factor, and that most fires occur POST CRASH or during HOT REFUELLING.

Most modern flight suits are made from a blend of Nomex material. NOMEX® IIIA is a blend of 93% NOMEX®, 5% KEVLAR®, and 2% P-140 fibers manufactured by DuPont. NOMEX® is a meta-aramid fiber that **doesn't ignite, melt, or drip,** and it retains its mechanical properties at elevated temperatures. KEVLAR® is a para-aramid fiber that has high tensile strength and is used to reinforce NOMEX®. P-140 is a static-dissipative fiber.

I am not advocating that you shouldn't wear FR clothing, if we mitigate all the risks associated of when helicopters catch on fire, then it is a bonus. The whole safety culture is about preventing it, as most of the time is human error. Even most authoritative bodies 'recommend' FR clothing, it is not mandated. Why? Because each helicopter mission is different, for an example, you are flying overwater and wearing an immersion suit. Yes, the material may be Nomex or FR coated, but the rubber/ latex seal around your neck and wrists most certainly isn't. It is all about Risk vs Benefit.

Set up a Flight Safety Committee and determine what your Team needs most. This does not replace the individual's right to where if they deem so. In our Peru aircrews, operating at high altitude and in extreme cold, the crews tend to wear a blend of modern mountain climbing equipment over a flight suit, this type of operation is covered in the Helicopter Crewman Essentials 'High Altitude/ Cold weather Operations' chapter.

If cold, add a jacket as it is easier to adjust your body temperature by adding/ removing external layers, than removing underwear.

Remember you are dressed for the conditions that you are flying OVER, not the conditions IN the aircraft.

Adjust the aircraft heater where you can to mimic the outside temperatures (may be difficult with a patient onboard) but adjust your body to what might happen when outside. Ever walked outside your house in the middle of winter or the hottest summer? We are trying to void that 'shock to the system'.

So, what do you carry in all those pockets? First item you should consider is a knife – not for slaying dragons, but predominantly for assisting YOU get out of the aircraft in an emergency.

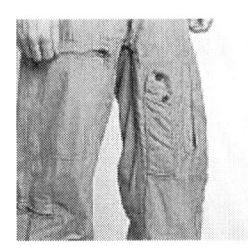

US Military style flight suits are fitted with a knife pocket (and lanyard) located on the left inner thigh. This was to house a simple lock knife; however more modern knifes can be included. I stress again this knife is designed for EGRESS (i.e. cutting seatbelts).

For those that do not have the knife pocket (or wear British flight suits), then an option that is available is the UK military aircrew ´J-knife´. Housed in a sewn pouch on either the left or right thigh and attached by lanyard. It is accessed distally, so that you can retrieve whilst seated more easily. Has an annoying point that you can extend to emergency deflate lifejackets (or cut yourself!).

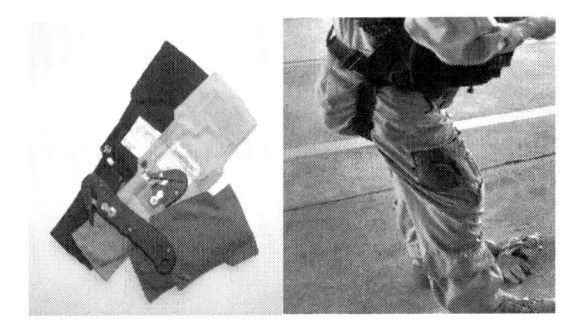

A good egress knife I have used is made by Benchmade ®, It has replaced my Trauma Shears as they are that good. I have it in a secondary pouch located on the center line of my survival vest, and have added a home-made red bead handle for easy opening:

So, we are dressed in our flight suit that is bristling with pockets, what else can fit in there?

Many a post on various social media is about Medics carrying a ton of med gear, yes and guilty myself in the past, now limited to a reference book, medical gloves and maybe a couple of syringes. Med kit goes in the med bag!!

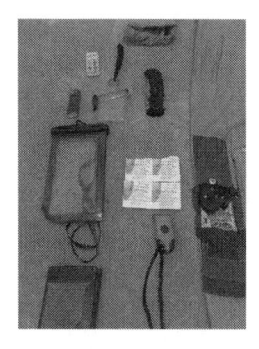

Items worth considering are:

- Baseball/ sun hat
- Fire lighting steel, butane lighter
- Mosquito Head net (can double as small fishing net)
- Dry tinder for firelighting
- Solar phone charger/ LED light and cable
- Unlubricated condoms for water collection
- Whistle

- LED Microlight
- Paracord

And remember the <u>Mandatory</u> aircrew survival items – Credit Card, phone charger and sunglasses!

What is not common (for example in the USA) is the use of hi-visibility clothing. In the UK for example, the HEMS crews tend to wear blaze orange with reflective tape so that they are easily identifiable. The black Wolf SAR crewmembers wear a custom designed two-piece suit by StephanH, specifically for this reason. It is bright blue (for easy recognition), has a removable fleece liner as well as knee. Elbow protections plus a specific back protector (for hoist operations. The reflective stripes do three things:

1. Allow you to be more visible at night
2. Enable you to conform to aviation safety laws of wearing Hi-visibility/ reflective clothing on the ramp/ flight line
3. Allows the crewman in the helicopter to see which the crewman's arms/ and legs is due to the different number of stripes.

Boots

A highly personal choice, dependent on your program and local regulations these may need to be of a certain standard and construction.

Before starting with a new program, it is always worth checking. For example, on our aircraft we do not permit steel toe caps at all (stems from us all being ex-military where steel toe caps were prohibited as you can kick/ damage the aircraft and not know you have done it) and have you ever tried either swimming with full flight gear and 2 extra pieces of metal attached to your feet, or going through a local Customs and Immigration……..

Although like I say, this is our company policy (we tend to wear desert or mountaineering boots). The aim is to be comfortable, for the duration of your shift, and in the event, you end up making a forced landing and need to walk anywhere.

Lights

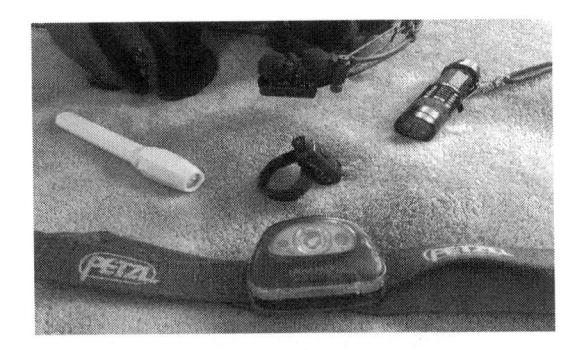

There a many commercial sources of light available, from torches to head torches. There are two types that are specifically designed for helicopter pilots that may prove advantageous.

Lip Lights

As in the description, these are mounted below your microphone and operated with your bottom lip pressing the switch on/ off. A cable leads to a AAA battery pack that is secured to the back of your helmet with hook and loop tape. Available in a variety of LED colors, depending on your mission. Mine in the picture is 2 NVG friendly green and 1 IR LED light.

Finger lights

Designed for pilots to illuminate the control panel, or whilst consulting navigational charts, finger lights can be an excellent addition. They have a simple hook and loop strap that wraps round your finger, and the on/ off switch is operated by usually your thumb.

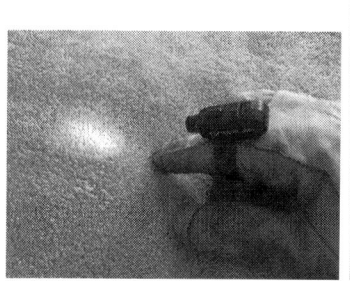

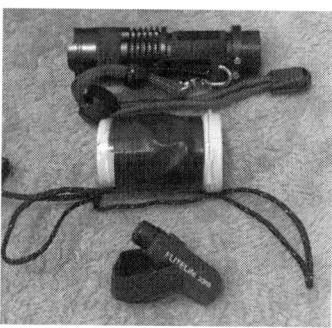

As they are quite small, and easily lost, a perfect container to keep them in (if not supplied) is an old Blood Glucose Tester lancet container. As with everything a lanyard attaches it to wherever you wish to keep it when not in use.

Normal torches

Whether a separate head torch or hand-held model, always carry a normal torch. For walking to and from a scene of injury call, or simply for the pilot to do his Preflight walk round (when they forget their own). I personally use the Surefire 'right angled' torch, it clips to the center of my vest and is very small. It replaced the old-style military 'right angled' torch, but unlike those (if anyone ever has used them) this works when you turn it on....

Glasses

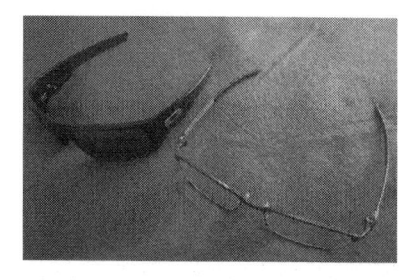

For sunglasses or regular prescription glasses, a better ear cup seal can be obtained with frames that end in a bayonet style as opposed to the normal 'behind the ear' curve. Normal frames can be worn, but dependent on your helmet/ headset type they can cause very uncomfortable pressure points after protracted periods of time, plus they can be very difficult to put on/ take off whilst wearing a helmet/ headset.

The United Kingdom Civil Aviation Authority (CAA) offer the following guidance aimed at Pilots specifically:

Frame choice

All frames should be well fitting and comfortable. The choice of frame should minimise any effects on peripheral vision. The eye size should not be too small and a frame with a reasonably thin front (e.g. metal) and sides should be used. However, for those pilots that may have to use emergency oxygen, such as commercial jet airline pilots, the sides of the spectacles need to be strong enough to be placed under the oxygen mask straps.

For presbyopic pilots/ATCOs with good uncorrected distance vision, reading glasses should be in a ½ eye (look-over) style of frame. A full frame reading correction is unacceptable. If a full frame is preferred to ½ eyes, a multifocal lens must be used.

Ballistic goggles

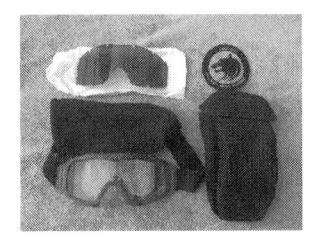

Ballistic goggles you all say!! For the current/ ex-military aircrews reading, if you have ever flown in a 'dusty/ sandy country', even with the advent of the MFS face shield, a large amount of dust can sometimes still blow up the inside of the screen and your visor. Goggles can be an effective way of protecting your eyes, depending on your helmet visor style, on some models you can still close the visor with the goggle's underneath.

GoPro camera

At Black Wolf helicopters, we film everything. We have a written policy on filming firstly before everyone complains, but why do we do it? It allows video debriefs, a visual record of search operations and for training purposes. The cable pictured, allows the GoPro to record both internal/ external communications via the ICS cord.

Night Vision Goggles (NVG)

Once upon a time (not so long ago), even the military aircrews did not have Night Vision Devices (NVDs).

In 1998, A Royal Navy Lynx from 815 Squadron Fleet Air Arm (UK), Flew into the South China Sea off southern Singapore during a night surface exercise which included engaging targets while operating off HMS Grafton. The aircraft sank and the salvage operation was conducted by the Royal New Zealand Navy. The pilot escaped with minor injuries, but the observer was killed. My friends.

One of the prime reasons for this fatal crash/ ditching? Before the advent of NVGs, Pilots and observers had to turn down the instrument lighting to avoid instrument glare on the windows. A caveat however, NVG operations conducted by the military are TOTALLY different to those conducted by civilian organizations.

Night Vision devices increase the aircrew's situational awareness, ability to safely navigate, however, also can dramatically decrease the associated risk.

In comparison to daylight operations, they do have operational limitations, including reducing a user's depth perception, which is an important factor during external work such as hoist operations. While operating NVG's it is difficult to identify suspended wires, which are also difficult to see day or night. The goggles themselves have a narrow 40°field of view (smaller than the normal human binocular visual field of 120° [vertical] by 200° [horizontal]) , however since they are suspended over an inch from the eye they do not restrict the user from looking below the goggles or peripherally to the side in order to perform an unaided task. Originally in the 'Green' form you are all familiar with, NVGs now are progressing to white phosphor. The advantage of white phosphor in image intensifiers is that it exploits the efficiency of the human visual system in processing black and white images.

Depending upon the probability of detection of a missing search subject, a SAR helicopter may consider delaying a search mission until darkness in order to increase their chance of success. This is based upon NVG's being able to detect any light source, helicopters fitted with Infrared (IR) or Forward Looking Infrared (FLIR) may also prefer this option due to the increased contrast in temperatures.

It is also very important to learn how night vision goggles are used while flying at night. The correct operational use of NVG's is a necessary safety component of aviation goggle training. Training in the use of aviation goggles occurs initially in the classroom and is then transitioned to a flying environment

NVG Non-Pilot Crewmember Training Requirements FAR 135

The following guidance is provided by the Federal Aviation Administration as the minimum training required to act as non-pilot crewmember in an aircraft whilst using Night Vision Goggles (NVGs) under FAR Part 135. The rule outlines Ground training requirements.

FAA Order 8900.1 Training Program Requirements (NVG Part 135)

In addition to pilot crewmembers, the additional crewmembers (e.g., flight nurses and EMTs, who perform duties in flight, are required to have an approved training curriculum. This training includes:

- Five hours ground training that must include one hour of NVG demonstration and use, which must be accomplished at night and may be accomplished in flight or on the ground.

- These crewmembers will receive the same ground training segments as the pilot crewmembers, including the aircraft specific and operator specific segments. CRM will be emphasized during crewmember training.

Pre-flight preservation of night vision

- **Sunglasses (NV-15)** a lens with a VLT of 15% allows that much of the visible light to pass through the lens and reach your eye (it blocks 85% of the light).Unfortunately, most of the sunglasses offered (including the most expensive) do not publish their UV, IR or Visible light transmission levels. The only guide I can offer for you to judge on your own is to find a pair of Ray-Ban© sunglasses with the G-15 Grey/ Green lenses and look through them, they have had a VLT of 16% for over 40 years. The Randolph Engineering Military Issue glasses with the Neutral Grey lenses (Dark grey) also have a 16% VLT. If they are good enough for 'Maverick'....

- **Adjust cockpit lights** (military aircraft are fitted with specific NVG filters in order to provide no visible/ external light from the aircraft)

- **Adjust inside and outside lights**

- **Close one eye**

- **Supplemental oxygen**

- **Avoid brightly lit areas**

- **Nutrition**

- **Hydration**

DARK ADAPTATION

- It takes approximately 30 to 45 min. for complete adaptation.
- Can take up to 3 to 5 hrs. if exposed to the glare of snow, water, or sun.
- Red lens goggles decrease dark light adaptation time.

SCANNING TECHNIQUES

- **Stop-turn-stop-turn technique.**
- **Ten-degree circular overlap.**
- **Off-center viewing.**

VNEs

- NOE - 40 kts
- CONTOUR - 70 kts
- LOW LEVEL - VNE or whatever ambient light, weather conditions and experience dictate.

COST

Not cheap equipment, but an investment that is well worth it for safer night operations:

- ANVIS $10,747.00
- CARRYING CASE $ 29.47
- V1 MOUNT $ 197.00
- LIF'S $ 80.22
- BATTERY PACK $ 200.67
- 25 MIL LENS $ 337.67
- IMAGE INTENSIFER $ 3,363.28

Components of ANVIS

Goggles

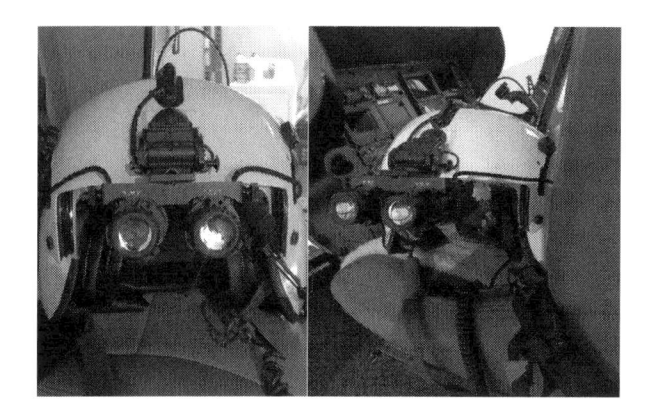

Power pack assembly

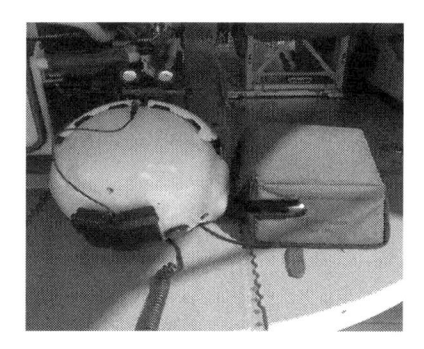

1. Power pack assembly - The assembly provides power for the ANVIS using Lithium or AA batteries.
2. 2. The original power pack accepts only BA-5567/U lithium batteries and draws the power for the low-battery indicator from the compartment opposite the one being used to power the ANVIS.
3. The dual-battery type of power pack accepts either two BA-5567/U lithium batteries, four AA alkaline batteries, or a combination of one BA-5567/U lithium battery and two

AA alkaline batteries. Power is drawn for the low battery indicator from the compartment with the highest voltage. There are two types of dual-battery power packs.
4. Type 1, identified by the suffix -G1 or -G2, produces a steady illumination of the low battery indicator light on the visor assembly.
5. Type 2, identified by the suffix -G3, produces illumination of a blinking low battery indicator light on the visor assembly.

Counterweights

1. The recommended initial weight is 12 ounces. Add weight or remove weight to achieve the best balance and comfort. **THE WEIGHT BAG SHOULD NEVER WEIGH MORE THAN 22 OUNCES.**
2. Weights should be of the ROUND 'shot' type
3. Attachment of the weight bag should be low on the back of the helmet with the battery pack mounted vertically above it.
4. The adjustment of weight in the weight bag should be made with the binoculars attached and flipped down.

IR Strobes

A common misconception, the filter is only there so that people with NVGs can see you. Special Forces, downed aircrew or tactical units do not operate at their best whist illuminated by flashing lights! The filter shields the strobe flash to the naked eye, so you do not necessarily need one of these types!

These strobes have 3 settings,

1. IR shield – only visible to those wearing NVGs
2. Normal – The IR shield is removed by hinge to expose a normal strobe light
3. Blue filter – The green plastic outer casing is pushed 'upwards', this puts a blue plastic filter of the normal strobe light but shields the flash. The blue filter is there to allow the individual to point the strobe directly at the rescue helicopter. It is blue so cannot be mistaken for weapon muzzle flashes by military helicopter door gunners.

'A Day in the Life' by Aaron Sheldon MPH Candidate, BS, FP-C, EMT-P

I live approximately 10 miles from base, and it takes about 20 minutes to arrive. My shift begins at 1800, but I have always made it a habit to arrive an hour early, an old habit I picked up in the Navy. If the team I am relieving is not out for a ground run, then I begin my looking the aircraft over. I usually start at the nose and work my way around the helicopter, ensuring all the connectors are connected, Zeus fasteners are fastened, and panels closed as they should be.

After a thorough walk around I inspect the gear within the aircraft which consists of a Hamilton T-1 ventilator, a Zoll X-Series monitor, a monitor bag with basic essentials for assessing blood pressures, electrodes, transducing arterial lines, esophageal temperature probes, as well as thermometers, and end-tidal capnography equipment (side stream and inline). Other items in the aircraft are Baxter infusion pumps, survival equipment, the intravenous line starting equipment, warmed crystalloids, and blood warmer for our blood product, which consists of plasma and packed red blood cells.

Additionally, our helicopter is outfitted with a case for the night vision goggles, two goggles are inspected by the medical aircrew, and one is inspected by the pilot. I usually check these after I complete my interior and oxygen level checks. This is an essential step in the process. Many times, goggles go unnoticed until they are needed, and then when the crew mounts them, they find battery issues, or the goggles are out of adjustment. This not only slows down the aircrew but makes you an unsafe member of the team.

After the aircraft check is finished, I check our tech bags, which we carry on both ground critical care runs and flights. It contains a load of different types of equipment. A checklist must be used when going through the bad. Each compartment has its own specific purpose, and once an aircrew person is familiar with bags, he or she can find exactly what they are looking for in a hurry. Once the bag is checked, I check our balloon pump, ventricular assist device bag, and last the narcotics. After everything is accounted for, an electronic check sheet is signed for and emailed to the respective leadership people.

Around this time, I check my helmet bag and helmet to ensure that the night vision goggle mount is intact, the chin strap is ready to go, and the overall durability of the helmet is safe for flight. I then make my way to the paramedic room and change into my flight suit. Our base has a very high volume, so getting "toned" out for a run is common. Sometimes by "rotor," sometimes by ground.

If we get a flight, and it is dark, which at night it usually is, or will be by the time we get lifted or close to our destination, it is critical to set up the night vision goggles and ensure they are functioning correctly on your helmet, I try to always accomplish this task inside the lighted hangar. Usually, at a smaller base, this can be performed during routine aircraft checks, but our base has three teams who all use the same night vision goggles. Which means I cannot mount mine and leave them on my helmet. That said, this requires a few extra minutes of mounting and then dialing in the goggles, so it is possible to see clearly at night. If goggles are not dialed correctly in, vision can be blurry and cause headaches.

I ensure all our gear is onboard and secured, I place the narcotics in my right lower leg pocket and pack the blood and plasma with cold packs. I assist with pulling the aircraft from the hangar, chock the dolly wheels, and perform a second walk around. I usually take my seat in the left forward cabin next to the pilot and assist with finding frequencies to our destination and any hazards associated with landing there. The pilot begins the start process, and I watch gauges to be sure all is well. Once the aircraft is started and ready to lift, we perform closed-loop call outs that include placing mobile phones in airplane mode and maintain a sterile cockpit for lifting. The area begins to lift, and my eyes are out the left side, scanning for obstacles. Once the aircraft is at cruising altitude, I continue to scan but also assist with radios, and depending on the length of the flight, I call the receiving hospital for assurance that the pad is secured. If it is a "scene" flight, I will find the radio frequency and wait until we are within line of sight to raise them for a landing zone report.

As long as the flight is under visual flight rules (VFR) I spend some time preparing for the patient. Mainly this consists of communication with my partner and a brief review of protocols. If I suspect the patient will need rapid sequence induction or a weight-based medication, I write the calculations down and compare them with my partner. Once everything is confirmed, it is ordinarily smooth flying from there. Landing is dependent on whether or not the patient is from a hospital or scene. Hospital landing zones are reasonably benign. However, it is still critical to keep eyes out.

Scenes, on the other hand, require a lot of attention to detail, and all hands must be eyes out, calling out every hazard possible in order for us all to keep the Pilot informed.

Once the aircraft is safely on deck, we make our way to the rear of the EC-145, remove the cot and our gear. We make our way toward the patient and take over care of the patient. This is regardless of a scene or not. The only difference is that the scene our aircraft may remain hot (rotors spinning) while we transfer the patient. This is a time-saving method, but at any time, safety becomes a concern. Our rotors will be shut down. After the patient is stabilized, packaged, and ready to go, he or she is moved to the aircraft and secured by a kingpin and straps for added security. A noise attenuating headset is placed over the patient's ears, and we prepare to lift. The same process as before, except in this instance, one crewmember stays with the patient and once does a walkaround to ensure the aircraft is safe for flight.

Once back inside, I plug back into the intercommunications system, and we go through the call-offs again. After call-offs are complete, we lift and head toward the hospital. Care is continued once the aircraft is at cruising altitude. This is difficult because I am so used to patient care that I find myself trying to perform care instead of looking out for obstacles, but time has taught me always to be scanning for obstacles and other aircraft. Depending on flight time, we manage the patient, and approximately 10 minutes out from the receiving facility, we call and give them a patient report.

Once we land and have determined where in the hospital we are going, we make our way to the correct floor. Still monitoring the patient and trying to make sense of all the tangled lines. Care is ultimately turned over after the report is given to the bedside staff, and we clean our cot and gear, wrap up everything, and restock items used during the transport. Finally, we make our way back to the aircraft and reload our equipment, perform a walk around, remount night vision goggles, and lift for the base.

Most of the city hospitals are less than five minutes from the base, so our transit time is short. We land on a dolly and park the aircraft back inside the hangar, not forgetting the post-walk around and debrief. We then chart and wait for our next run, flight, or whatever challenge awaits us. Usually, I run two to four runs in a shift and wrap my shift up around 0600.

If, for whatever we have free time, I spend some of it resting, studying, and reading. If the opportunity arises, I eat and drink lots of fluids just in case. This is an old Navy habit of mine, just in case I fell overboard and was missing for days. Each team at the base has a specific house duty, but as most things go, no one supervises, so it sometimes gets done and others, it just gets forgotten or avoided. I try and keep my area and gear clean despite the house duty I am assigned. I am kind of a loner at work and like to spend my time away from the other teams focused on reading and blog writing.

That is really a day or instead night in the life of a critical care/flight paramedic in the helicopter EMS world I currently work. I like it, I do not love it. I am more of an active person and need more adrenaline. I love learning the critical care side of things but otherwise feel like my hands are tied, and we are limited to flying a really fast ambulance with basic and antiquated resources. Maybe one day, I will find my calling. Until then, I smile and show up bright and early for every shift, do what I can to make our patients lives better, and go home at the end of the day.

Take away:

- Flying is exciting but dangerous
- Logistics are difficult (loading a patient into the helicopter is not easy)
- Night vision goggles are critical to safe flight but training on use is essential, more importantly having designated pairs for every crewmember might reduce time and mistakes
- Utilizing checklists for both gear checks and pre-flight are important and necessary
- Pre and post briefs do not get discussed enough due to logistics and crews coming in at different times
- Educating crew members on not just what to look for but how to look for obstacles is critical
- IM SAFE should always be used, however, rarely gets discussed, crews are too proud

Survival Kits

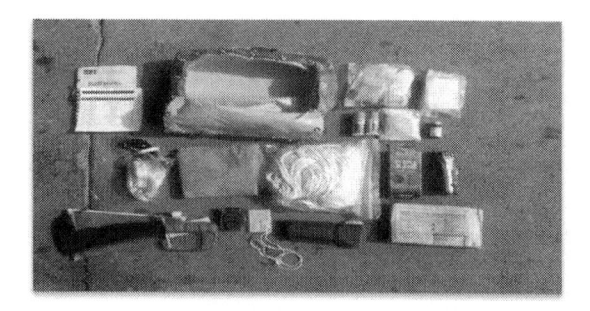

The aim of a survival kit is to give you the tools to enhance your chances of survival. They vary in many sizes – from a large aircraft jungle survival kit, to a small personal tin. Depending on your location and weight restrictions, it may be as simple as a knife and a Firestarter.

Survival tins

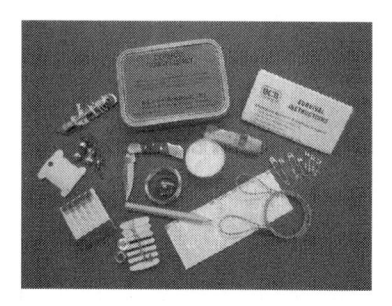

The ´Combat Survival tin´ is a very popular choice for many people. Designed originally by the British Special Air Service (SAS), it is designed to sit in a trouser or jacket pocket. If the soldiers had for whatever reason discarded their rucksacks or webbing equipment, then they still always had their tin on their person.

They contain a few simple items that with the correct knowledge assist in the priorities of survival. They can be commercially bought or home-made.

Survival vests

Designed for aircrews, the survival vest is an excellent and comfortable way to carry survival equipment. Extensively used by military or civilian aircrews, based on the statistical fact; In the event of a crash ¨if it isn't fastened to you – you won't have it´.

Vest types can range from complete whole-body vests with built in life preservers as pictured, or to smaller chest platforms, with modifiable pouches for custom fit.

Whatever method you utilize it needs to be small, compact and lightweight (so that you get accustomed to always carrying it on your person). If you decide to build your own, some items for consideration to include may include:

- Small folding knife with locking blade
- Fire lighting steel, butane lighter, matches and small candle
- Mosquito Head net (can double as small fishing net)
- Dry tinder for firelighting
- Unlubricated condoms for water collection
- Whistle
- LED Microlight
- Paracord

- Small fishing kit
- Snare Wire
- Safety pins

It is easier to build a generic kit that applies to all over the world, and then expand your individual knowledge on how to survive more effectively using your kit in the climatic region you are visiting.

This chapter will now look at some of the simplest methods of Land Survival that apply to most countries, or methods that can be modified according to local plant life and foliage. The aim is to give an underlying knowledge on which you can further develop through training.

PROTECTION

Shelter can protect you from the sun, insects, wind, rain, and snow, hot or cold temperatures. It can give you a feeling of well-being. It can help maintain a will to survive. In some areas, the need for shelter takes precedence over the need for food and even the need for water. Always dress according to the conditions that you may face in any environment. If you are cold walking to your car or the airplane – you are not dressed correctly!

If you don't have the benefit of an aircraft to sleep in, the most common error in making a shelter is to make it too large. A shelter must be large enough to protect you but small enough to contain your body heat, especially in cold climates. Make individual shelters, rather than a large one (that will probably collapse) that is less thermally efficient.

Try and choose a site for your shelter that ´feels nice´ if possible. If your location feels cold, it will get colder! Avoid riverbeds due to the risk of flash floods and insects the converge on stagnant water.

You may have an emergency sleeping bag / survival shelter in your kit, which are only useful for short overnight survival before they get damaged. Utilizing the resources found in nature, a far more robust shelter can be established. The type of shelter will depend on a variety of factors and considerations.

Take the following into consideration:

- The time and effort needed to construct the shelter – the most energy you have will be NOW.
- Will the shelter provide adequate protection from the elements?
- The type of materials needed for the shelter

Rather than confuse yourself, learn 2 types of shelter, that you can practice in whatever environment you find yourself in.

´One for areas where you need to be off of the floor (for example the jungle) and one ´for everywhere else´.

These can be manufactured from any materials available to hand with the right knowledge.

Lean-To

The lean-to shelter is probably the easiest and quickest type of wilderness shelter to build and is suitable for most terrain. It can be built as complex as you require and with materials readily available in nature. The jungle lean-to pictured was built in approximately 2 hours by a student on a survival school in Guatemala with only a machete. The Lean-to does require 2 things:

1. A cutting tool,

2. An abundance of building materials

Always build this type of shelter with its back to the prevailing wind.

- Place two Y-shaped sticks about 4 feet long and bury one end in the ground, so they stand about 3 feet high. Take a long branch about 6 feet, as a ridge pole. Lay the ridge pole between the two forks. The lean to can be made more secure by using whatever materials might be available to tie the ridge pole in place
- Next take several other sticks and lay them across the ridge pole, securing them in place will assist in making a sturdier shelter. The opposite end can either be buried in the ground or have large rocks placed on top of them to assist in holding them in place. This will provide the basic skeleton of the shelter
- Cover the skeleton with whatever material is available. Natural materials can be used but should be layered from the bottom to the top. This provides a thatching that will keep water from dripping into the shelter.

This shelter is perfectly suitable from everywhere from the jungle (as it raises you from the floor and protects from rain) or to Arctic Circle conditions (with the addition of a parallel fire – without a sleeping bag you can sleep comfortably in temperatures as low as – 50 degrees Celsius).

Thermal A-Frame

A very simple and highly effective thermal shelter (for one person), the Thermal A-frame allows you to survive cold temperatures if you are unable to make fire.

This shelter is also easily constructed with basic materials. It is easily warmed and provides protections from both wind and water when properly built.

- Mark out the length of your body on the ground with 2 sticks/ rocks to give you the length.
- Create an "A" for the tent door by resting sturdy diagonal branches opposite each other that meet where head will be.
- Place a long sturdy pole to serve as the ridgepole into the "A", and check that your body fits into the framework. Use vine, thin green branches or rope to lash together all support points
- Create a ribbed frame with branches set along the ridgepole, wide enough so you have room inside.
- Cover from ground up with any thatching material that you have available; dead leaves from the forest floor, Bracken, Leaves, Snow – as long as you cannot see daylight through your thatching (Fig XX).
- Improve the Thermal characteristics of this shelter by manufacturing a ´door´, once inside – close the door, and your body heat is retained inside the shelter more effectively.

Insects!

The most effective insect repellents usually contain a high concentration of DEET-based solution which is safe to spray or rub onto your skin and on your clothes. If you don't have this but can find a citrus based fruit to rub its juices onto your skin, which can work too.

Clothing should cover your arms and legs and the darker colored and thicker the clothing the better.

However, you should always check your clothes and footwear and shake them out before putting them on, especially if you've been airing or drying clothes outdoors. Likewise, with any sleeping bags or blankets you may have – give them a thorough shake and inspection before using them. The smoke from your fire is also a good way to keep many insects at bay. However, as one of the many skills needed to survive, is accepting that you are a visitor in their home!

Fire

In many survival situations, the ability to start a fire can make the difference between living and dying. The importance of being able to make fire cannot be stressed enough. It pertains to all the 4 priorities of survival, and is what made the Homo sapiens the top predator on the planet:

1. PROTECTION – Keeps you warm preventing calories being used to generate heat, keeps insects and wild animals away, cut large logs when no cutting tools available, provides mental comfort and be a psychological boost by providing peace of mind and companionship

2. LOCATION – Allows signaling to aircraft and rescue teams

3. WATER – To boil and purify water, to create a desalinator to make sea water drinkable

4. FOOD – Cooks raw meats and makes certain plant species edible

Basic Fire Principles

To build a fire, it helps to understand the basic principles of a fire. Fuel (in a nongaseous state) does not burn directly. When you apply heat to a fuel, it produces a gas. This gas, combined with oxygen in the air, burns. Understanding the concept of the fire triangle is very important in correctly constructing and maintaining a fire.

The three sides of the triangle represent air, heat, and fuel. If you remove any of these, the fire will go out. The correct ratio of these components is very important for a fire to burn at its greatest capability. **The only way to learn this ratio is to practice**.

FIRE SITE SELECTION

The location of your fire is one of the most important steps undertaken when constructing a fire. If a proper location is not found, then you will make your job infinitely more difficult. Find a place that is out of the wind and elements, that will have ample fuel, and that doesn't cause a hazard. It's hard enough surviving in a forest; it's even harder trying to survive a forest fire! The more you do in preparation before ever striking a match, the easier it will be to start and maintain a fire. Make your fire as small as possible... you'll use less wood, and therefore less energy. If you're using the fire as a signal, you can keep it small, yet have a prefabricated signal fire ´pyramid´ structure ready for immediate notice and use.

FIRE MATERIAL SELECTION

To build a typical fire you will need three different types of materials; tinder, kindling and fuel. Before attempting to start a fire, remember;

´PREPARATION, PREPARATION, PREPARATION´

Tinder is dry material that ignites with little heat--a spark starts a fire. The tinder must be absolutely dry to be sure just a spark will ignite it. If you only have a device that generates sparks, charred cloth will be almost essential. It holds a spark for long periods, allowing you to put tinder on the hot area to generate a small flame. You can make charred cloth by heating cotton cloth until it turns black but does not burn. Once it is black, you must keep it in an airtight container to keep it dry. Prepare this cloth well in advance of any survival situation and add it to your individual survival kit.

Tinder Examples:

- Cedar bark
- Dry wood shavings
- Dead grass, Straw dead moss, dead ferns
- Cotton wool (can be enhanced with Vaseline)
- Dead pine needles or similar
- Sawdust

Kindling is readily combustible material that you add to the burning tinder. Again, this material should be absolutely dry to ensure rapid burning. Kindling increases the fire's temperature so that it will ignite less combustible material.

Kindling Examples:

- Small twigs or small strips of wood
- Cardboard
- Tree bark

Fuel is in the form of larger pieces of wood to make it bigger and in order to it to keep it burning for longer. The materials you choose for fuel should be less combustible and should burn slowly but steadily.

Fuel Examples:

- Dry, standing wood and larger branches
- Insides of dead tree trunks as long as they're dry
- Bunches of dried grass
- Dry peat often found near riverbanks
- Dried animal dung
- Pine tree knots containing resin Fuel
- Coal

Collect all of the materials you require prior to attempting to start, it is considered best practice wherever you are to lay a foundation ´platform´ of wood that you build the rest of the fire on. This protects the flame from cold or wet ground and provides additional fuel to your fire.

How to Start the Fire

There are many different ways of lighting a fire. Some of these methods date back many thousands of years although they can often take months, if not years, of painstaking practice to learn. Even modern-day fire-steels need practice on how to use effectively, as with everything in survival, there is a ´right way and a wrong way´.

You may have several ways to ignite a fire in the survival kit but a review of basic fire building and starting principles is important as well as some of the more primitive ways to start a fire. Before considering the 'ignition' element of the fire making process, you should have prepared yourself.

Therefore, you should have ensured that you have at least one, but preferably two, sources of fire igniting equipment contained within your emergency survival kit. Always ensure that you have collected your tinder, kindling and a good-sized portion of your fuel before starting the fire off. The tinder is the first material you'll light and as it's the most delicate, it's better to light it upwind. To make things as easy as possible, you should either use a lighter or some matches.

Lighter and Matches

Dampness can affect lighters however and matches should be waterproof and kept in a waterproof container. If these fire starters are the only fire starting tools you have, you should treat like them like 'gold dust' as you cannot be sure how long it will be before rescue reaches you, so try to work off the principle of 'one fire, one match'. Alternatively, if you've a candle or strips of rubber inner tube in your survival kit, this may cut down on the number of matches you use. Lighters can still be utilized if empty, all you need is the spark mechanism to work!

Using a Lens

As you are harnessing the powers of the sun, this method can only be used during daylight hours when it's sunny and bright. Your lens might come from various items of equipment you might have brought with you – a camera, glasses, binoculars, a magnifying glass or broken glass. In fact, you can even use water in a clear plastic bag or ice with the correct knowledge and technique. Whatever type of lens you use, you should angle the lens so that it concentrates the rays of the sun directly onto the tinder. Hold it over the same spot until you can see that the tinder is smoldering. Then you need to gently blow or fan the tinder until it bursts into flame at which point you can add your kindling.

Using a Battery

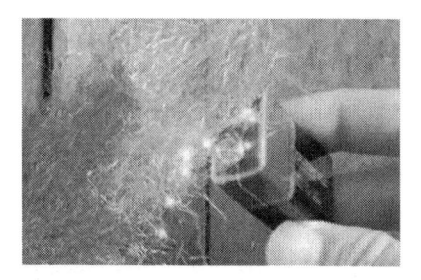

Even a simple AA battery, in fact most types of batteries, can be used to light a fire. All you need is to attach a piece of wire or wire wool to each end of the battery and the touch the other ends of the wire together next to the tinder. This will create a spark which can be used to ignite your fire. If you know your helicopter, you will know where its battery is stowed!

Fire-steel

The direct spark method is the easiest of the more ´primitive´ methods to use and more importantly it will still work if the equipment itself is completely wet. There are many different types, from the type pictured above with a striker and steel, the US Military type with a block of magnesium to provide tinder and one-handed compact models. The fire steel method is the most reliable of the direct spark methods, although this method requires some practice. When a spark has caught in the tinder, blow on it. The spark will spread and burst into flames.

Fire by Friction

There are many different methods of fire by friction, and all require knowledge and constant practice on how to construct the necessary pieces of wood in order to be successful. Some examples are,

- The fire-plow
- The fire-bow
- The bamboo saw

You rub a hardwood shaft against a softer wood base. The rubbing action of the various types creates small particles of wood fibers that progressively heat from friction until they reach their combustion point. This hot ember is then transferred into a kindling bundle.

TYPES OF FIRE

There are many ways to lay a fire dependent on what you want to achieve, and these are 4 examples of the most common used:

A ´Pyramid´ fire

The simplest and easiest fire to construct and ideal for cooking with hanging pots or used as a base to develop further different fire types

A 'Star' fire

Feeding larger logs into a pyramid fire that is slow burning. Also allows to utilize larger logs that you are unable to cut.

A 'Parallel' fire

Uses large logs in conjunction with a shelter and fire reflector provides a slow burning, high heat to keep you warm from head to toe.

The 'log cabin'

A slow burning fire that is ideal for using with cooking pots. It also allows wet timber to be dried progressively

As described previously, the aim is to keep the fire as small as possible to be effective for its purpose. This is survival – not camping or having a BBQ.

LOCATION

The second of the Priorities of Survival (Protection, Location, Water, Food), but to me the most important!

You are not a survivor until rescued, and we all want to **go home**.

One of the biggest problems' rescuers face is where to actually start looking – if somebody knows you're missing at all!

If nobody knows you are missing, then nobody will look for you. Flight Plans (including CANCELLATIONS and UPDATES)/ Emergency Response Plans (and their dissemination to the correct authorities)) are key to maximize your chances of being found.

For ground-based operations in remote areas, key information for any pre-prepared rescue plan may include the following:

- Number and ages of persons in group, plus contact numbers
- Emergency 24/7 contact number of Point of Contact (POC) not involved physically on the operation.
- Equipment carried by group
- Level of training in outdoors environment.
- Start Time, Location and proposed route (plus any deviations from that route, example: 'This group is white water rafting River X, however on Day 3, we will trek to see the historic ruins at XX location before returning to the river the same day'). Even if a simple flight plan from point A to B, and you divert to C (even though only a few miles due to weather – how often does the pilot update ATC?).
- End Time, Location
- The groups intended actions in event of emergencies
- Any communications strategies (for example a communications schedule of calling a Point of Contact every 12 hours)
- At what point does a rescue plan need to be commenced?

This final point can be very important. If all your communications fail, and you have stated that at X time on X date – we are in difficulty somewhere and need help - then a plan can be swiftly put into place. If you are late through natural reasons, and communicate this as soon as practicable, then it is no problem. However, if you are stuck with a casualty, no communications, you will at least know that in X number of hours, somebody will start raising the alarm and your casualty management plan can be adjusted accordingly.

Use the ATC 'Flight following' service, a simple radio request that requires a pilot to inform ATC every 15 minutes that you are 'Operations normal':

1. **Callsign.** Use the full call sign until ATC shortens it. ...

2. **Type of aircraft**. They need to know the performance ability of your aircraft.
3. **Altitude**. If you are on their radar this info will help them identify you. ...
4. **Location**: this can be off an airport, VOR, fix or waypoint. ...
5. **Request**: Request VFR/ IFR flight following service.

An example of a ´Ops normal´ call is:

´ATC this is Medic 1, Currently Ops normal, 2 miles southwest of Big Rock Mountain, heading 120, 4 POB, 2 hours endurance, Over´.

Dependent on your local ATC procedures – You will have now have two options; fail to respond after 15 minutes and ATC attempt to contact you – SAR Services are notified or if you declare an emergency SAR will be immediately notified (as they know where you are!).

One of the many reasons to file a flight plan is to allow (in an emergency) people to start looking for you! A classic example here in Guatemala is a flight from the City to the tourist resort in Lanquin, a simple over mountain/ ridgeline flight of approximately 35 minutes. This is submitted as a flight plan, no problems, however!

If you get the time of day wrong and have to take the secondary route to avoid cloud base levels, this now takes you on a more North Westerly route, and increase the potential search area from a simple straight line search pattern to an area now approximately 7,200 square miles. Where does SAR start to look??

Simple message, don´t be shy – use ATC!!

Signaling

A disclaimer – this is purely my opinion on equipment based on my personal experience, please refer to your company procedures etc and if in doubt – ASK!

Wherever you are, you will need to signal your location at some point. Whatever you choose, remember most search aircraft look for color contrast – what ´doesn't look normal´ from the air for example. It is nearly impossible to see a human being from a search aircraft. The picture below shows a missing tourist (in red circle) from approximately 100 feet in the air, only spotted by the contrast of the sun reflecting from her inner arm.

There is a multitude of signaling options available, so this section of the chapter will look some of the common and simplest types available and more importantly those that can easily be transported through Customs and Immigration.

The Helicopter Essentials Aircrew Survival Manual will introduce some of the various types of equipment and its benefits / drawbacks; however, it is down to the individual to carefully select the equipment that works in their respective regions.

Many items (for example flares) are not permitted through Customs and Immigration without special permits and most flares can only be used once. Out of date flares need to be disposed of in accordance with local Governmental Authority Regulations, and for weight, durability and effectiveness there are far more effective devices available. To me on a personal side, apart from smoke flares at sea – there are far better devices available nowadays.

Aircraft equipment

If you are not a member of the flight crew (Pilot, Aircrewman or Crew Chief for example) – learn about how to use the radio in an emergency. Possibly you will not get chance whilst in the air – but once landed/ crashed (and the pilot incapacitated) it may well still work.

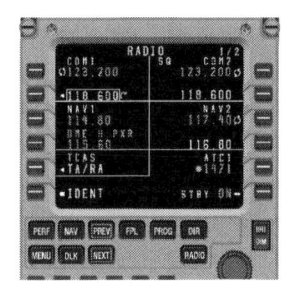

In ANY EMERGENCY, the priorities for the Pilot are:

´AVIATE, NAVIGATE, COMMUNICATE´

There are 2 types of Emergency call:

1. ´PAN´ - to declare a situation that is urgent, but for the time being, does not pose an immediate danger to anyone's life or to the aircraft itself.

    i. Example ´PAN, PAN, PAN......(Pause)...PAN. This is Medic 1, 5 miles southwest of Little Creek, currently showing Chip Warning light on my Starboard Engine, Returning to XX Airport´.

2. ´MAYDAY´ - to declare a life-threatening emergency.

    i. Example ´MAYDAY, MAYDAY, MAYDAY, (Pause). MAYDAY. This is Medic 1, 2 miles southwest Little Creek, Heading 210, 4 POB, Ditching´.

The Emergency frequency for all civilian aircraft is:

121.5 MHz

If you hear the term 'Guard' this originates from the military equivalent channel which is: **243.0 MHz**

IFF Transponder ('Squawk')

Originally designed by the military as a non-radar way of detecting Friendly Forces (hence 'IFF'- Identification – Friend or Foe'). Each aircraft is assigned an individual code by ATC, although there are specific codes for helicopters (as an example) operating either SAR or Ambulance tasks. This allows other aircraft to steer clear of you and maintain safety parameters. Unlike Radar (Radio Aid to Detection and Ranging), IFF is a simple encoded signal that is transmitted/ received by any other aircraft with a modern avionics' suite. It's how (Non-military) Air Traffic follow you. In the event of an emergency, the code is: 7700

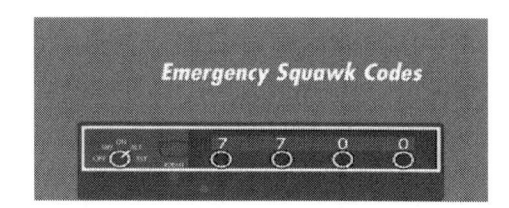

This is displayed as an emergency in ATC similar to the picture (military units that use active radar receive a different and more distinct 'eyebrow' around the target.

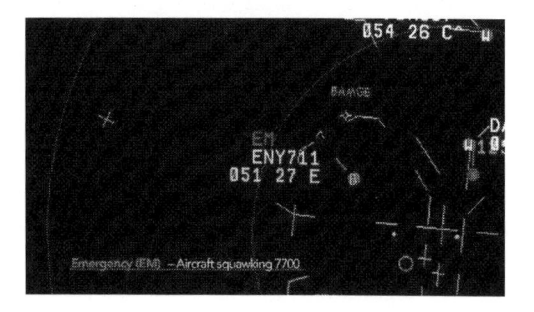

The aircraft ELT (Emergency Locator) is similar, and is either operated by a switch in the cockpit, or in the event of a crash is activated by the impact forces:

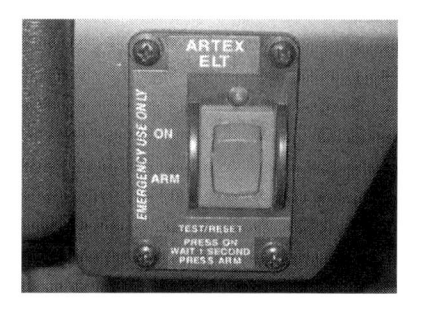

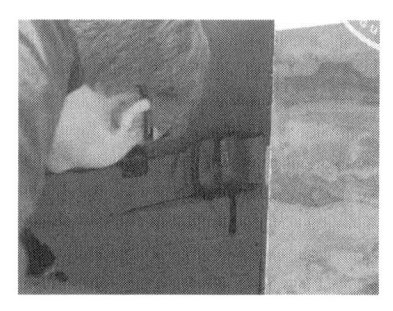

Ask the Aircrew/ ALSE team about they operate, it maybe you alone in the wilderness staring at the equipment at the end of the day...

All aircraft have many different emergency options, so it is really a case of spending a half hour learning about how they operate.

All my signaling gear is carried in the same pouch externally on my vest that I can access with either hand. Inside are two simple green cloth pouches that are there to stop everything getting ´tangled´.

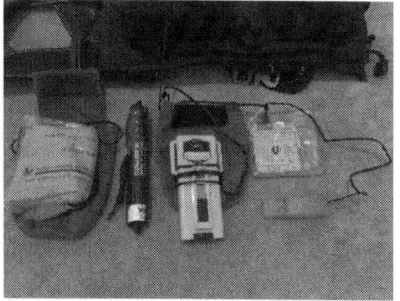

I personally carry, a PLB, an orange Ground / Air marker panel (which one day I will get manufactured in blue!), A Cyalume distress marker, ACR Strobe, Heliograph Mirror and Whistle, but we will take a look at some of the different basic location aids that you can carry, later in the Helicopter Essentials Aircrew Survival Manual, we cover those that are applicable for overwater operations.

A whistle

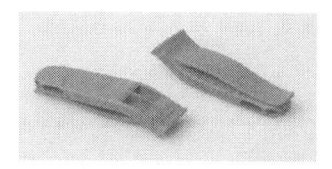

So simple and very often forgotten, there are many recorded instances of rescue teams walking past survivors who had lost their voices from shouting. Choose a whistle without a ´pea´ inside.

Fire

As mentioned, the most important of all skills to possess is the ability to make fire. Normal cooking and survival fires do not produce enough smoke to be visible from long distances or search aircraft. By constructing a simple signal pyramid, this can convert even a small fire instantly into a signal fire that creates large plumes of smoke.

- Place 3 sticks about chest height into the ground and tie the top together to create a pyramid or ´Teepee´
- Take smaller sticks and tie horizontally approximately 8 inches from the ground to provide a ´shelf´
- Line the base of the shelf with spare dry kindling, dry twigs and anything that will burn rapidly
- Above this layer, place green leaves, pine branches to create smoke
- On hearing or sighting a rescue team – lift the structure and place directly over your survival fire
- A more drastic/ effective method is to just set fire to a lone spruce tree – however be aware of forest fire risks!

Dependent on your backdrop you may need to change the color of the smoke to be more effective. In most areas white is enough, however in the desert or arctic regions Black smoke is preferred. This can be achieved by adding anything man made into the fire for example; rubber or plastic trash. White is Natural (For example if you fly for 10 minutes in Guatemala, there are campfires, forest fires in every direction. Each is subsequently investigated during a search pattern, however, Investigation = TIME.

Cigarette lighter

Obviously, a fire making device (even if empty utilizing the spark mechanism), but the spark itself can be seen by NVG´s over long distances (approximately 4 miles). So, a multi- purpose device!

Wire wool

Wire wool can also be used effectively at night, by attaching to a cord and lighted. If swung on the cord it creates a short acting signal device (similar time duration to a small firework, however, the more wire wool used, the longer it lasts).

Heliographs or Mirrors

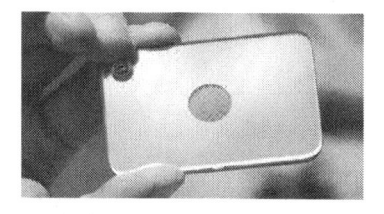

In the words of Tina Turner ´simply the best! ´. One of the best signaling items of all, and they can either be a purchased item or the inside of a survival tin lid kept highly polished. No moving parts, nothing that can break and visible for up to 24 km on a sunny day. They do require some practice in order to use them effectively.

Strobe lights

Highly effective at night, strobes are available in different styles and either operate manual with a switch or have an automatic function that operates the unit when in contact with water. Visible from approximately 5 km, some models have integrated batteries (with a shelf life of 5 years), others take standard batteries. The battery type depends on how long the strobe light will operate. The strobe on the right of the pictures is a military type with an Infrared Filter for NVG ops. These confuse many non-military people, so without teaching you to ´suck eggs´- the filter is only there so that people with NVGs can see you. Special Forces, downed aircrew or tactical units do not operate at their best whist illuminated by flashing lights! The filter shields the strobe flash to the naked eye, so you do not necessarily need one of these types! Many are fitted with a Velcro backing to attach to your flight helmet if in water.

Rescue Laser

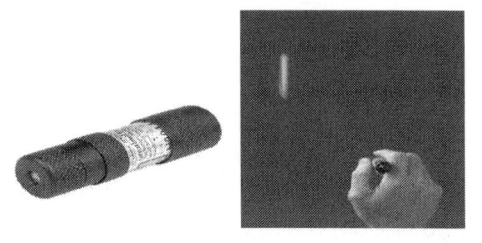

A relatively new device, the rescue laser when projected into the sky, gives an illumination area of approximately 6 miles that can attract the attention of passing aircraft. Unlike other lasers, this does not affect the eyesight of the Pilot and Crew. These lasers are specifically designed NOT to blind the aircrew, so unless you want you want your rescue helicopter crew sat next to you after crashing next to you..... Buy the correct and approved type!

Cyalume / Chemical Light Sticks

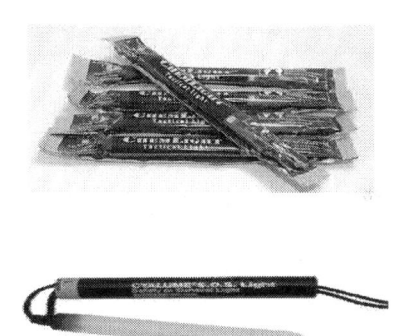

A very cheap and highly effective method of signaling at night, light-sticks can be used to mark individuals when walking at night, as illumination for shelters, marking paths and a multitude of other uses. With the addition of a length of cord and swung over the head in a rapid fashion they can be visible at night from approximately 2 miles (without NVG´s). These can be bought as a manufacturer purpose-built device or made you.

Personal Locator Beacons (PLB)

There are many different types of location devices available, from PLB´s (Personal Locator Beacons), modern PLB´s for example can transmit an emergency satellite signal that is accurate to 1.5 meters, however in developing countries there is no way of local rescue services accessing this information so if that is your sole Emergency communications plan then your system will fail. I have no affinity with any of the companies whose products are pictured (unless they want to send me a free one!). Quite expensive, but highly accurate, and if you operate in a region that SAR services can support it (unlike here!) – get one!

Surplus PLB/ SARBE beacons

These are available on eBay etc, and often look like a very cost attractive option. HOWEVER, they operate on the old 121.5 MHz satellite monitoring system (Not to be confused with the emergency distress channel). Approximately 6 years ago the US Government turned off satellite monitoring of this frequency. Modern PLB´s use the more effective 406 MHz – so simply, don't waste your money...

These are some of the basic devices that you should carry at all times. As with everything it can be paying a lot of money for something that you may (hopefully!) never use, but if you don´t have it, you can´t use it. A simple start is to make your sure that the initial flight plans, updates and associated procedures are in use, after that a few simple items that will aid you in attracting attention.

Items specifically for use at sea or in open water, are covered in a later chapter. This is when you really want to be found quicker than normal as the priorities of survival are much more difficult (but not impossible) to achieve.

WATER

Water is one of your most urgent needs in a survival situation. Crews can't live long without it, especially in hot areas where the body can lose water rapidly through perspiration. Even in cold areas, people will need a minimum of 2 liters of water each day to maintain efficiency; more than three-fourths of the body is composed of fluids. You must drink plenty of water even if you do not feel thirsty. The body loses fluid as a result of heat, cold, stress, and exertion. To function effectively, you must replace the fluid the body loses. So, after PROTECTION and preparing LOCATION signaling devices, one of the first goals is to obtain an adequate supply of water.

Before we fly however, we need to make sure that we are HYDRATED! A common problem amongst military aircrews is that of ´Tactical Dehydration´, crewmembers reduce fluid intake before flights to prevent the need to visit the bathroom. At the opposite end of the scale is over hydration: Urinary retention reduces attention span and our ability to make decisions to the same degree as alcohol intoxication or 24 hours sleep deprivation. So, as aircrews, we need to strike a happy medium and balance. The invention of hydration systems such as Camelbak, Platypus to name two commonly used systems, allows us to take regular sips of water over a protracted period.

SURVIVAL WATER SUPPLIES

As we always follow the ´dress to egress´ mantra, and that ´If it isn´t attached to you – you won´t have it´ over the years several commercially available options are available. These are in the simplest/ best and cheapest forms:

Surplus US Military water bottles:

A military 1-pint water bottle that was designed specifically to fit in a flight suit lower leg pocket.

Unfortunately, as green in color, remember (as with all equipment) to attach it to your equipment with a lanyard so if you accidently drop it....

Water Sachets

Water sachets are readily available, and when empty provide you with a container for further water collection, or a tin foil packet that with skill you can boil water and food in.

Sachets are available in small or large quantities, again place inside a Ziplock bag and attach with a lanyard to your equipment.

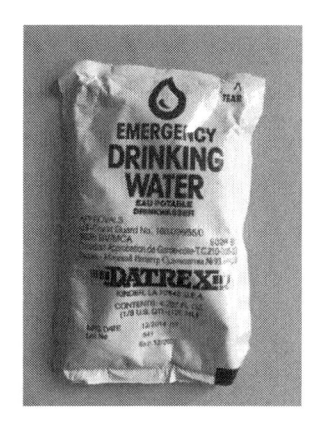

Your survival kit may come with a commercially made device for obtaining and filtering water; however, these may not always be available or may have become damaged during emergency landings. Therefore, it is important to have some basic knowledge of how to procure water in an emergency. I personally carry Ciprofloxacin tablets in my kit, so even if I get it totally wrong, I don't become too dehydrated through diarrhea!

BASIC WATER FINDING SKILLS: Finding water can be an essential skill to have. In much of the world water is plentiful. In mountainous areas, just continue to walk downhill and you will eventually find water. Watch birds and animals or follow their tracks they will usually lead to water as well. As is my usual method, rather than overload the reader with many ways, we will look at the simplest, and then after practice, the individual can develop their own further knowledge.

Medical supplies

You are a HEMS crewmember, whether a Paramedic, Nurse or Doctor, how do we treat a patient with chronic dehydration? If you have intravenous supplies that are not damaged, will let you work out what to do next. Rehydration and Continuous Professional Development at the same time…

USING THE EARTH TO FILTER GROUND WATER

The ground itself makes for a great water filter. If you are near a water source that is less than clean, simply use the ground to filter it. Go about 50 feet from the standing water, and dig. If the "pit" looks less than clean after water begins to fill it up, give it a few minutes, or continue to scoop out water and discarding until it clears up.

WATER FILTER FROM NATURAL MATERIALS

This filter is easily constructed using a variety of materials that should be readily available in. This filter doesn't filter down to viral levels* but is surprisingly effective, nonetheless.

Constructing the Filter

The filter can be housed in a hollowed-out log, a sock, rolled up bark, bottle or whatever else you can make a tube out of (a pant leg for instance) and needs 4 items:

- Item 1 is the crucial part. It is crushed black charcoal (not ash). This is wood that has been charred to black, and then crushed up to sand or powder consistency.
- Sand is packed on either side of the charcoal (Item 2).
- Grass, moss, leaves or other material is packed in to help retain the sand (Item3).
- Finally, a rock pushed into either end to hold it all in place (Item 4).

The rocks are not tight enough to seal anything; they simply keep everything in place.

You can skip both the grass and rocks if you have extra fabric to tie around the ends to hold in the sand.

Once the filter is completed, water is slowly poured in from the top and allowed to filter down through. The first few gallons of water that go through will be a bit murky. Discard this (or pour into a container for re-filtering) and keep pouring until the water clears up. We then need to refer to our most important survival skill – FIRE, to boil it. Water only needs to be brought to a rolling boil to make it safe.

*Note: Viruses are typically not an issue in water sources unless you are traveling into tropical regions. Most viruses found in the waters of N. America are bacteriophages. They are dangerous to bacteria such as Cryptosporidium, Giardia and other single cell protozoa.... which are the bacteria you're trying to get rid of anyway. If the charcoal layer is properly packed, this filter should trap the stuff you're primarily concerned about. In other areas, you will filter and then BOIL the water. The filter will take care of the murkiness, taste, etc and then the boiling will kill the rest.

Solar Still

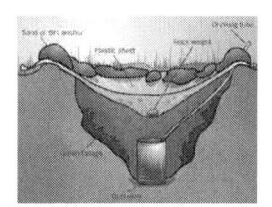

A solar still is traditionally what most people think of when trying to collect water in a survival situation. They are an efficient way to collect moisture from the soil but require a lot of effort (and potentially dehydration) to construct, compared with the amount of water they produce. After 2 – 6 hours, expect a small mouthful of water.

Constructing the Still

To begin construction, you must either dig a hole in the ground, or where this is not possible, build up the walls (which is less efficient). A tarp is then draped over the hole. This is sealed in place with rocks, logs, sand or whatever is available. Make sure it is well sealed. The sun on the tarp heats the air underneath, which causes moisture in the soil to evaporate. This moisture has no place to go and condenses on the tarp itself. A pebble placed in the middle of the tarp will provide enough of an angle so that the moisture will run to the center and drop into a collection vessel.

Notes:

- The collection vessel can be anything... cup, bowl, tin can, another section of tarp, even a large leaf.
- The drinking tube shown in the pictures is a nice addition, but not necessary. You can always lift the corner, reach in and remove the collection vessel every so often. It's more work, but if all you have is a tarp, then it may be necessary.
- If available add in vegetation to the base. It doesn't even matter if the vegetation is edible or not, as you are effectively distilling the water.
- The evaporation process can be speeded up by urinating on the vegetation (not into the collection cup!).

The water that is collected from a solar still is 100% pure, drinkable H_2O, and does not require boiling.

Tree still

By far my favorite method – a very efficient and less work intensive method is to utilize a tree still. Simply find a non-poisonous plant with lots of green leaves, place a bag over a branch and tie the bag shut around the branch. As the sun heats the day condensation will form and the bag fills with water. By adding a length of plastic tubing (think length of oxygen mask tubing etc.) into the bag you can drink directly without breaking the seal.

Intravenous fluids

Using the process of de-salination, we can produce drinking water from our IV fluids (Normal Saline or Lactated Ringers being the better tasting), with either direct sunlight or fire.

Both methods need you to practice first so you understand the concept whilst in a safe environment. To put in simple terms, we are going to take the 'steam/ condensation' from a hot liquid and cool it in a tube to drink. The direct sunlight method is rather slow (as with everything in nature). Take a normal fluid administration set, spike the bag as normal, but cut the tubing before the distal end/ injection ports. Lay the bag 'upside down' (fluid ports upwards) at a slight angle, and solar heat will cause condensation to form in the tube, where it will drip slowly into your collecting container.

Using your fire is very similar but a fsater process, this technique is ideal for sandy regions as we can elevate the fire. Using our same IV components:

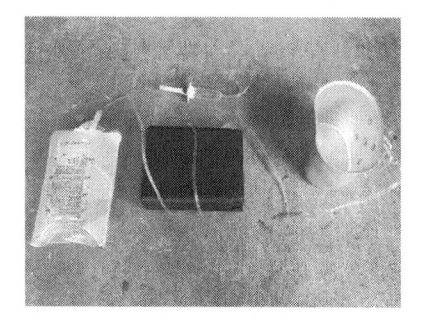

The IV bag (or any container containing liquid including both sea water and urine), is placed on or near the fire. If the bag is full it will boil and not melt, steam evaporates into the tube, and is then cooled before running into our cup. Tubing is normal IV tubing with the spike chamber removed.

Early morning dew

Easier still! A very easily forgotten method of water collection, find any area with long grasses early in the morning, wrap spare clothing around your ankles and simply – walk.

As the moisture collects into the clothing, stop and squeeze collected water into a container before repeating the process, a very easy method that is so often overlooked.

Urine

If you drink urine, then you have a choice: Dehydration or renal failure. Simple.

There are cases of people surviving a short period of time drinking their own urine, but these are very few. A way in that you can drink urine, is to boil it, collect the steam in a condenser and drink that (as that is 100% water), however in the absence of a tubing, containers and such in a survival situation, the only real option is to build a solar still and urinate into that. But as described there are far more efficient means of collecting water that rely on you using less energy to construct.

Finally, there is a lot of reference (especially in the movies), of water rationing. It is NO GOOD in a container, you need to drink, remain hydrated and allow your body to make conscious decisions in the attempt to secure more water.

Water is our third Priority of Survival, but if anyone has ever been thirsty......

FOOD

When faced with a survival situation people almost always begin to think about food. Hunger pangs are highly likely to 'kick in' if you are stranded for some time without food but it's important to remember that you can actually survive for 3 weeks without food as long as you have enough water to sustain you. You probably won't be very happy or fit, but you will be alive. Therefore, food is the last of the priorities of survival, you need to abide by the rule of 3's and obtain protection, location and water – whilst you have energy to do so.

Rations

In order to reduce the risk of eating a potentially deadly/poisonous food all crewmembers are encouraged to carry some small amount of emergency food in their vests. These are readily available commercially and the best forms (with longest shelf life) are those supplied for Liferafts and Aircraft Emergency Kits. They usually contain a vacuum sealed bar and dependent on type contain approximately 2500 calories each.

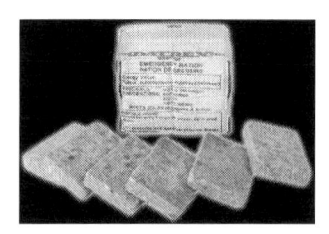

Carried by Aircrews since WW2, and available on Amazon for Liferafts etc., another option can include a simple tobacco type tin containing hard boiled sweets that you can coat for extra energy with ´baking sugar´.

These can be used in a couple of ways, the first and most obvious is to just put it in your mouth, or you can empty the tin out, and now you can boil water with a sweet added and have a morale boosting drink. If you also add common cooking ´stock cubes´, either meat or vegetable stock and some salt sachets, you can include these into any wild food concoction that you make, to make them more palatable.

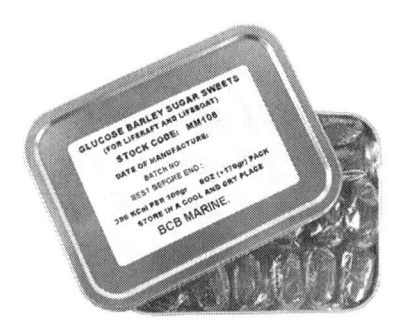

As with all our equipment, you must employ a regular system to check the date and seals on any food that you carry in your equipment.

If you find yourselves stranded for an extended time period and feel that you need to source food in order to survive there are some general guidelines below you can follow. Take time in the environment that you operate to consult local specialists who can assist you in learning local food sources.

Plants, Berries and Fungi

These are probably the most difficult category to determine when it comes to considering whether they are safe to eat, and it cannot be emphasized enough that you should not eat anything that you cannot 100% identify.

Certain plants can poison on contact through skin absorption, by ingestion or inhalation through the respiratory system. These include hemlock, castor bean and castor oil plant, oleander, lantana, poison ivy, poison oak, death lily and many varieties of fungi which can be lethal. This list barely scratches the surface, however. The only way to be sure is to do the research and find out what plants are growing in the location you're heading to and learn how to identify those which are safe to eat.

The military over the years has developed what is known as the ´taste test´ as consuming even a small amount of a toxic plant can cause gastrointestinal problems, or even death. Survival experts devised this test to determine a plant's edibility. It is a slow process, but each step is necessary. (Warning: This is for emergencies only. Plan A should always be to positively identify everything you eat.)

1. Separate the plant into its various parts—Focus on only one piece of the plant at a time.
2. Smell it. A strong, unpleasant odor is a bad sign.
3. Test for contact poisoning by placing a piece of the plant on your inner elbow or wrist for a few minutes. If your skin burns, itches, feels numb, or breaks out in a rash, don't eat the plant.
4. If the plant passes the skin test, prepare a small portion the way you plan to eat it (boiling is always a good bet).

5. Before taking a bite, touch the plant to your lips to test for burning or itching. If there's no reaction after 15 minutes, take a small bite, chew it, and hold it in your mouth for 15 minutes. If the plant tastes very bitter or soapy, spit it out.
6. If there's no reaction in your mouth, swallow the bite and wait several hours. If there's no ill effect, you can assume this part of the plant is edible.
7. Repeat the complete test for other parts of the plant as some plants have both edible and inedible parts.

It is not 100% foolproof though, so no matter how abundant and tempting plants and berries might be, you should never eat any wild vegetation unless you are 100% sure you can identify it.

Pine needle tea is one of the easiest ´foods´ to produce, and one of my favorites (as it involves the words TEA).

It contains 4 to 5 times more Vitamin C than freshly squeezed orange juice and is also high in vitamin A and is so simple to make. Chop pine needles then add to hot water and drink....

Like all survival skills, try and learn 2 or three edible plants that are common in your region and practice!

Insects

I will spare the audience from the pictures! Whilst insects may not be the first choice on your menu, they are usually found in abundance and are the easiest kinds of 'meal' to find. They provide you with a very rich source of protein and can be made more palatable by adding into soups, stews or broths (another reason to carry stock cubes!). You can eat most insects raw if preferred but always remove wings and any barbed legs first, me personally I either dry for a day in the sun or cook and grind it a powder before adding to a soup. Although common worms with scrambled eggs is particularly nice!

Fish

There are no poisonous freshwater fish so you can eat them safely, but you should cook them to get rid of any parasites first. They can be caught in several ways from traditional ´line and lure´ (if you carry in your kit obviously) to using your head net as either a gill net or a simple fishing net. Fishing lines have been used for centuries in the UK manufactured from natural cordage (nettles) and plant spines (such a Hawthorn for example), add a modern touch and make the float out of one of your foam earplugs!

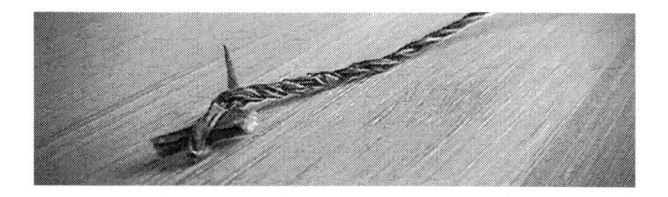

Amphibians

Most species of frog are safe to eat but you should avoid eating any brightly colored ones or those which have a distinctive X mark on their back. However, frogs should not be confused with toads which secrete a poison if they're in fear of an attack. Toads tend to inhabit drier areas than frogs.

Birds

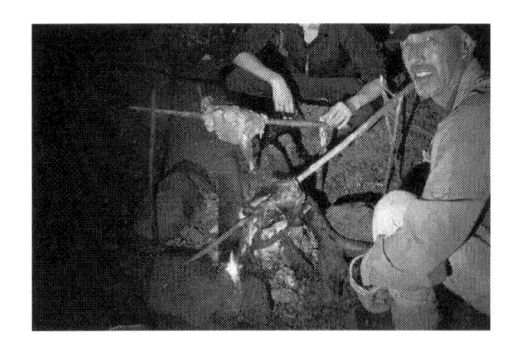

All bird species are edible although the taste varies tremendously. Catching can be very difficult, the easiest method is a long length of thin cord (approximately 3 feet) with fruits or similar threaded along its length. With one end of the cord anchored to a tree, ground feeding birds ingest the cord as the eat the berries, when they try to escape the cord is securely wrapped within the GI tract and they are unable to escape. Other methods can include a mesh laid over the birds feeding ground to ensnare their feet, to a simple loop snare (which is where the name ´Booby trap´ originates! From the traps used to catch the Booby (sea bird).

What birds do provide (if you can find them of course) is EGGS! One of the ingredients for your worm omelet!

You can cook in two other ways, if you don´t have a cooking pot, in the campfire ashes:

Or in a large ball of Sphagnum moss (or large ball of wet grass):

Mammals

All species of mammals are edible however scavenging mammals can often carry diseases, and it is important to think ´how much energy will I expend catching this animal, compared to the nutritional gain I will receive (If you manage to catch it at all). Mammals also pose the risk of the survivor encountering injuries as it defends itself. Snares and traps are the most effective means of capturing animals. Unless you are lucky and have experience in poaching or hunting for most of your life. Don't expect to catch any mammals.

Food is the final of the Priorities of Survival, but one that all people think of first. Terence MacSwiney an Irish political prisoner in 1920 lasted 74 days on a hunger strike before his death.

One of the key human factors is survival food is being able to adapt to what you can gather without the benefits of modern spices and flavorings. Many people have died not being able to adapt or overcome their own individual dietary beliefs or ability to eat food in its purest forms. **Hiroo Onoda continued to survive in the jungle unaware that WW2 had finished**

for 30 years, he stated that he could not afford to be concerned with whether he "liked" any of the food he obtained. He just ate it all.

As a sobering reminder, just remember all the living things mentioned, will quite happily eat you.

COLD WEATHER AND HIGH-ALTITUDE FLIGHTS

Flying at high altitude brings us another set of challenges that we need to prepare for as part of the survival culture. Unfortunately, it is not a case of going out and buying the best mountain sleeping bag, tent and assorted paraphernalia. Why? One word, WEIGHT.

For us to fully understand this as crewmembers, we need to first understand another key term 'Density Altitude'.

Many search and rescue operations requiring helicopters occur at times of high temperature, high humidity, and often at high elevations (subsequently low atmospheric pressure). Unfortunately, each of these three variables negatively affects the performance of a helicopter.

Density altitude is the effect on aircraft by these three variables (temperature, humidity and atmospheric pressure) although increased humidity has only a minor affect, on density altitude.

A helicopter cannot work as effectively at higher altitudes as it can at sea level. The effect of increased temperature would be the same as increasing the elevation to which the helicopter must now fly. On a hot day, the density altitude at a single location may be 2,000 or even 3,000 feet higher than the elevation of that location on a cool day. The higher the density altitude, the weaker the helicopter performance.

Density Altitude is calculated using a formula, either on a flight computer or other software since the advent of computers by the Pilot before Take Off.

So practically what does this mean to us a crewmember? At High Elevation, performance is reduced because the thinner air at high-density altitudes reduces blade efficiency. This, in turn, requires additional pitch and power to maintain the same lift capability. The greater pitch angle results in increased drag that requires additional power.

The more weight we carry = the more power we require from the aircraft.

Dress to Egress

All the principles still apply in order to dress correctly still apply, although we need to think of the terrain that we are going to be flying over. In cold weather or mountainous terrain, any crash scenario is likely to be a protracted affair as search times find us, combine this with (especially in SAR missions, the doors will be open to aid visibility) and it gets cold very quickly.

Often people over emphasis the risk of fire in crashes, when as mentioned earlier the leading cause of death in helicopters at 86% is blunt trauma. So, you are protected from fire, but freeze to death.

Even the UK Military SAR Teams operating in Scotland wore fleeces, and mountain climbing Gore-Tex jackets as part of their dress to egress procedures.

Many people still do not realize that Flight Suits are available in summer and winter weight, so that is the first start point. Then purchase a quilted flight jacket and if you WEAR it, you are already on the right track. Many people complain that they are then too hot in the aircraft, so open a window or turn down the heater! We are at work and this is essential PPE, so overcome these problems.

I personally use an Ex- UK military two-piece quilted flight suit, under which I where a base layer then a fleece layer. My personal preference is a fleece body warmer style as then you don't over restrict arm movement.

An aspect that is often overlooked as many people fly in the same boots all the time. For crewmembers we need to consider that unlike the Pilots, we will be moving around, maybe getting out of the aircraft, so our footwear needs to reflect the environment we are operating in. From classic style mountain climbers' boots, to fleece lined Mukluks, wear what is comfortable and suitable for what you are doing.

Aviation Life Support Equipment (ALSE) / Individual Survival Kits

As a basis is our clothing, and then a survival vest. Like water egress, if the helicopter is about to roll over the cliff edge, you will get out as soon as the opportunity arises. So, our survival vest is yet again key to our chances of survival. The same multi environment equipment that we always carry, EVERYWHERE. We may add in for example an emergency pair of sunglasses, thermal balaclava, specific to our region. If solely operating at High Altitude, we may remove the water for example, as we can procure this from snow or ice by melting it in our head net for example and use the space we have created for specific regional items.

If purely low level and winter operations, then if our weights and balance permit, each crewmember often carries a mountain style rucksack, with potentially Snowshoes, a winter sleeping bag, Bivvy bag, stove and specific cold weather items etc.

If we are operating at High Altitude though, this may not be an option. All you have is what you are wearing and your vest. If the full crew can't fly adequately dressed to egress, then as part of the mission risk assessment – REFUSE TO FLY! Start looking at alternative options.

Helicopter Crew Oxygen

Federal Aviation Regulations and Oxygen Use (Title 14 of the Code of Federal Regulations)

Sec. 135.89 Pilot requirements:

Use of Oxygen. (a) Unpressurized aircraft. Each pilot of an unpressurized aircraft shall use oxygen continuously when flying—

(1) At altitudes above 10,000 feet through 12,000 feet MSL for that part of the flight at those altitudes that is of more than 30 minutes duration; and

(2) Above 12,000 feet MSL.

At night, because vision is particularly sensitive to diminished oxygen, the FAA recommend using supplemental oxygen when flying above 6,000 feet MSL

Types of Oxygen Equipment

Helicopters will either have a built-in oxygen system, or portable cylinders (usually in bags on the back of seats), and the most common form of delivery is through a Bi-nasal cannula. Often found also in the aircraft are the small Pulse Oximeters, so that crews can access their saturation levels. Of a newer design, especially for crewmembers who may have to move around the aircraft, exit to recover casualties etc are portable devices.

Our Black Wolf Helicopters Crewman in Peru use either a Bi-nasal cannula, or a normal O2 mask (no bag fitted and just visible underneath the Maxiofacial screen).

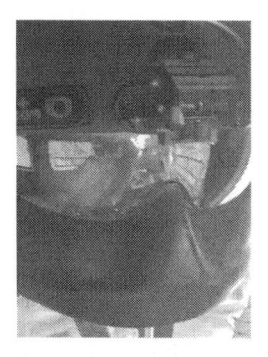

The system is connected to a demand flow system that is adjustable dependent on user's needs.

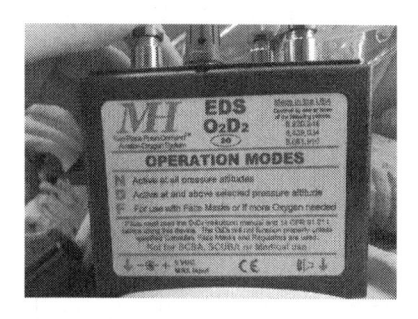

One similar device by Capewell Aerial Systems (USA) is the PHODS (Portable Helicopter Oxygen Delivery System), developed for the US military, and is a smaller Oxygen bottle that allows crewman to move around with less restrictions.

Whatever system you operate with, as with everything it needs to be checked (Pre-flight and Post flight).

For oxygen systems we can use the 'PRICE' Check

The acronym PRICE is a checklist memory-jogger that helps pilots and crewmembers inspect oxygen equipment.

PRICE CHECK	
PRESSURE	Ensure that there is enough oxygen pressure and quantity to complete the flight.
REGULATOR	Inspect the oxygen regulator for proper function. If you are using a continuous-flow system, make sure the outlet assembly and plug-in coupling are compatible.
INDICATOR	Flow indicators may be located on the regulator or within the oxygen delivery tube. Don the mask and check the flow indicator to assure a steady flow of oxygen.
CONNECTIONS	ensure that all connections are secured. This includes oxygen lines, plug-in coupling, and the mask.
EMERGENCY	Have oxygen equipment in the aircraft ready to use for those emergencies that call for oxygen (hypoxia, decompression sickness, smoke and fumes, and rapid

	decompressions.) This step should include briefing passengers on the location of oxygen and its proper use.

OVERWATER FLIGHTS

This chapter of the Helicopter Essentials Aircrew Survival Manual concentrates on the equipment that may be necessary when we add open areas of WATER to the survival equation. Each of the Priorities of Survival (Protection, Location, Water and Food) still need to be addressed by the crewmember, but now in what is a ´hostile environment´.

Our life is easy! Survival equipment for overwater flights is defined in the FAA Federal Aviation Regulations (FARs) SS 91.509 (2019 issue) as:

Survival equipment for overwater operations.

(a) No person may take off an airplane for a flight over water more than 50 nautical miles from the nearest shore unless that airplane is equipped with a life preserver or an approved flotation means for each occupant of the airplane.

(b) Except as provided in paragraph (c) of this section, no person may take off an airplane for flight over water more than 30 minutes flying time or 100 nautical miles from the nearest shore, whichever is less, unless it has on board the following survival equipment:

(1) A life preserver, equipped with an approved survivor locator light, for each occupant of the airplane.

(2) Enough liferafts (each equipped with an approved survival locator light) of a rated capacity and buoyancy to accommodate the occupants of the airplane.

(3) At least one pyrotechnic signaling device for each liferaft.

(4) One self-buoyant, water-resistant, portable emergency radio signaling device that is capable of transmission on the appropriate emergency frequency or frequencies and not dependent upon the airplane power supply.

(5) A lifeline stored in accordance with § 25.1411(g) of this chapter.

BUT.

You flight program doesn't do the FAA definition of ´overwater flights´?

This picture is here in Guatemala over Lake Atitlan, if we had an aircraft emergency...

Question yourself, based on the picture:

- Where is the safest and flattest place we can land?
- Which gives <u>us as a crew</u> the best chance of survival?
- Not necessarily an overwater flight, but water is our only real option of a safe landing...

After our initial escape from an aircraft ditching, we immediately need to focus on the following:

1. Airway Management
2. Thermal Management
3. First Aid (stop bleeding and preventing Marine predators coming for a free dinner)
4. Group Management

If we are correctly ´Dressed to Egress´, we can eliminate everything but emergency first aid (which we can still achieve), and the equipment we wear all aids in LOCATION.

But for you to be able to use any of this equipment, you need to be able to GET OUT.

The first reported helicopter ditching occurred on November 1st, 1944. Second Lt. Jack Zimmerman had to dive down to extract Private Troche from a flooded R-4 Sikorsky helicopter.

No one paid much attention to deaths in helicopter ditchings until 1971 when Glancy reported that in 55% of ditchings the cause of death was drowning/lost at sea. In 1973, Rice and Greear then reported that in 40% of their case study, the cause of death was drowning/lost at sea.

Finally, in 1978, Cunningham reported on 234 helicopter mishaps between 1963 and 1975.

His significant findings that the survival rates were:

66% without dunker training

And

91.5% with dunker training.

The leading cause of death is DROWNING.

In a study in 1978 it was found that in a study of 196 deaths, 37 drowned even though they were not injured Drowning was also blamed for 56% of civilian and 80% of military deaths in Clifford's 1993 report to the Civil Aviation Authority

The fact is that if you ditch in a helicopter there is likely a 15% chance that you will not survive…

Why?

Up to 15G crash forces, explosions as cold water hits the hot turbine intakes, rotor blades shattering, and helicopters do not float well. The majority (85%) invert almost immediately and then sink rapidly at a rate of 9 – 13 feet per second. If you exit too soon, you have rotor blades to contend with.

Also don't forget "cold shock" if the water is below 15°C (59 Degrees Farenheight). It has been proven I trials that that breath holding ability is reduced by 25 – 50% in water below 15°C. (59 Degrees Farenheight). In 0°C (32 Degrees Farenheight) water, most people can only breath hold for 12 – 17 seconds to make their escape.

Unless you have received underwater egress training, whatever you think you would do. WILL KILL YOU.

In this part of the Helicopter Essentials Aircrew Survival Manual, we will look at the procedures that need to be taken, in order for you to survive the impact, and then egress. It must be emphasized that you need to receive pool training to do this effectively.

Firstly, as with every flight we need to 'Dress for Egress':

Lifejackets

If you don't wear a lifejacket and end up in the water. You will die. Period.

The aim of a lifejacket is simply to keep your airway clear of the water even if unconscious (as opposed to a ´Personal Flotation Device (PFD)´ of the style that kayakers' wear. Lifejackets are fitted with water operated lights/ strobes, and as with an immersion suit, not only save your life, increase your visible surface area above the water.

They can be a ´constant wear´ aviation specific type, or like those that you see on commercial airliners. Constant wear is designed to decrease stress on your neck, and prevent your helmet causing damage by the constant rubbing. I currently use the ALPS collar from P1 Air Rescue, and it is not noticeable at all (compared to my life of older military styles) as the rear section is located out of the way of my helmet.

Whatever model, its needs to be of a MANUAL inflation. That means you as the operator pull a cord or inflate with your mouth. AUTOMATIC, and SEMI-AUTOMATIC will inflate as soon as the activating mechanism contacts with water (a cardboard 'washer', prevents the spring-loaded pin from puncturing the CO_2 bottle). Result, you die pinned inside a sinking aircraft.

They do have one drawback. When fully inflated and worn correctly, if there is any waves, they turn you to face them. This then causes you to ingest water, so if your lifejacket isn't fitted with, keep your flight helmet on, visor down, if fitted (and if you still have it) replace the Maxillofacial Screen (MFS)/

If you don't wear one already for whatever reason, now is the time to wear a vest. Apart from it holding your lifejacket, HEEBDs it holds signaling and survival gear. When helicopters sink. They SINK RAPIDLY.

Any illusions of you recovering your survival bag from inside the aircraft are slim to zero. That's if that part of the aircraft is still there.

My Aircrew survival vest is set up so that anything needed whilst in the water is mounted EXTERNALLY.

On the left side of the vest is mounted a secondary J Knife, an Individual First Aid Kit (IFAK), SEA MK2 HEEBDS bottle and SeeRescue Streamer.

The right side of the vest contains a vacuum sealed aircrew survival kit (for land use), a SOG Revolver knife (stowed in the saw mode, to aid in aircraft escape if required), and a signaling equipment pouch.

All location equipment carried for land survival can also be used at sea. Some are repeated here but I recommend that you read all the chapters!

My set up has all of my signaling gear in the same pouch externally on my vest that I can access with either hand. Inside are two simple green cloth pouches that are there to stop everything getting ´tangled´.

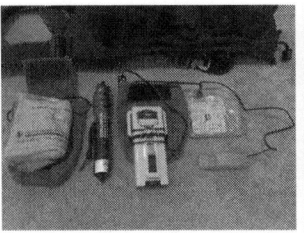

If not learnt already, now is the time to make sure that everything in your survival vest is ATTACHED TO YOU. If you drop it in the water, well......

Immersion suits

Immersion suits should be worn when the water temperature is below 15°C, or any extended helicopter operations over water. Not only do they increase your in-water survival time up to a potential 19 hours (with correct thermal protection underneath), their natural buoyancy, forces a more supine position in the water, therefore increasing the surface area of your body above water.

Usually available in orange, they come in a multiple color (well, orange and yellow, black/ dark blue or khaki to allow tactical/ military capabilities), however even the ´tactical models´ i.e. I have the Mustang Constant wear suit; these have separate high visibility hoods and inflatable mittens in pockets, with the neck seal designed to be less painful than more traditional models...

Whatever immersion suit you use, take your wristwatch off FIRST and remember after donning, you need to squat down and 'purge' as much air out of it as possible (usually by slightly opening the neck seal). Then replace watch strap over the wrist seal/ glove or in some suits, they have a mid-thigh strap that you can attach a watch to if you so desire. As latex seals are tight, it is common to dust the inside with powdered French Chalk, or non-aromatic Talc (the same as used for babies).

So, as a MINIMUM we have a Lifejacket, and dependent on our mission profile an immersion suit.

But going back to our 'Rule of 3s' we need to add another item to this equipment. Essential in cold water 15°C (59 Degrees Farenheight) and recommended all the time by most.

It is vital to have some form of air system for helicopter underwater escape, especially flying over water below 15ºC. They provide approximately 2 – 2.5 minutes air (8-21 breaths), and is your body, USE IT – WHEN YOU NEED IT!

Whether it's the STAS (Short Term Air Supply) HEEDS/ HEEBDs (Helicopter Emergency Egress (Breathing) Device type with the mouthpiece attached to the bottle, or the SEA bottles, with different length hoses connecting to the mouthpiece, there are many different types available, but all need training to use.

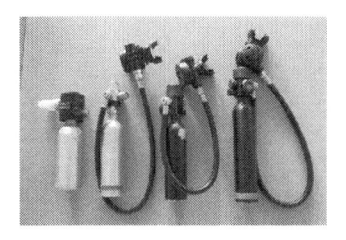

The first problem you experience is that your sinuses are full of water (which is not pleasant), so you need to learn to BREATHE to clear this water. This is not a normal reaction.

Secondly, due to Boyles' Law it now becomes interesting! On exiting the sinking aircraft, if below 5 meters, neither your lifejacket nor air trapped in your immersion suit will provide enough buoyancy for you to float as you will be 'Negatively buoyant' so you need to SWIM to the surface. Combined with this as you are swimming towards the surface, as you are breathing compressed air, you will need to exhale, or you will receive severe barotrauma to your lungs.

We are now dressed for any emergency ditching event, but what we need to remember from the outset that we are DITCHING and not CRASHING. They both end up in the water, however, back to our rule of 3s.

'3 seconds following a bad decision'

Crashing is totally unforeseen and a result of human error due to the circumstances at the time (usually a combination of speed, visibility and low altitude). A mistake is made and the next thing we know, we are in a washing machine on full spin.

For all other ditchings, is usually either a mechanical failure for example, or at least we receive notice of what is potentially about to happen. So that gives us two distinct options:

1. UNALERTED – For example, mid-flight over water and we hear the helicopter main gearbox whine and 'fall apart', we weren't expected this to happen, but we know that we each a few seconds to prepare.

2. ALERTED – We are having a really bad day, are over water and about to run out of fuel. The Pilot shuts down one engine, but it is only a matter of time before the remaining engine 'Flames out' due to fuel starvation. This may be in 3 minutes, 30 minutes or 3 hours, but we have time to sit and prepare and position ourselves for egress better.

Before we look at the different actions to be taken, we need to talk about the part of the brief on a commercial airline that EVERYONE IGNORES!

Why is that pertinent for us as crewmembers? I guarantee that you would listen to the brief to the person dressed on the left, as opposed to the right picture.

Airbus A320, US Airways Flight 1549 departed New York City's La Guardia Airport on 15th January 2009, when they suffered a double engine bird strike, that culminated in a successful ditching on the Hudson river.

Of 160 passengers, only 36 had got their lifejackets out of the packaging, ONLY FOUR PUT THEM ON! Of the 2 people that entered the water, neither were wearing a lifejacket.

So, as part of our safety culture, to support the Pilot we should promote those around us listen to the briefs, as one day, you will be potentially doing the passenger brief!

The BRACE positions.

Why do we do this? As I have personally experienced ditchings more than once, a ditching can exert up to 15G of force, with water hitting equivalent to a fire hose. In a study by the United

Kingdom Civil Aviation Authority (CAA) in 1995 on a crash of a Boeing 737, of the total 126 'Persons onboard (POB)':

- 39 were killed
- 74 survived (with serious injuries)
- 5 had only minor injuries

The brace position was analyzed especially and was ultimately found to have significant effect on injury patterns and outcome.

So, what does the BRACE position do?

A poor crash position will cause your arms and legs to flail, and you may be injured, so highly unlikely that you will be able to unfasten your seatbelt. The result is that you will drown. You need a good crash position to:

a. Reduce strike envelope;
b. Stabilization in seat to reduce disorientation;
c. Minimize body profile to inrushing water; and
d. Smaller human target to debris

However, the BRACE position <u>changes</u> dependent on how you are seated in relation to the aircraft, there are recommended positions detailed by relevant individual Aviation Authorities, however it is commonly accepted in most legislation that *'In the case of an unplanned emergency, the flight crew may only have enough time to give a short command such as "lean over" or "grab your ankles." Experience has shown that an attempt to take a brace position of some sort, the passengers will end up in a position which could result in less injury than if no attempt had been made at all (FAA):*

In general:

Forward Facing:

Visor down, ICS cable disconnected, Upper body - bent forwards at the waist, both hands support the head, In the case of front seat (Pilot co-pilot seats), hands should grasp the shoulder straps (thumbs out or they will be dislocated) with chin placed into neck, legs should be inclined aft of the vertical and feet flat on the floor.

- Aft Facing

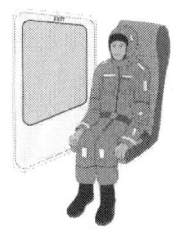

Visor down, ICS cable disconnected, Place chin into neck, grasp seta with both hands, legs should be inclined aft of the vertical and feet flat on the floor.

- Side Facing

Visor down, ICS cable disconnected, hand nearest to reference point placed over back of neck for protection and to allow instant point of reference (egress point) direction. Spare hand under back of legs (for protection). Legs should be inclined aft of the vertical and feet flat on the floor.

We are dressed correctly, we are in the correct BRACE position, what happens next?

A classic line from the movies is 'in space, nobody can hear you scream', in a ditching:

'No one can hear you scream, or tell you what to do'

As discussed, previously there are two types of ditching: Alerted and Unalerted,

So, we will look at each in order, first is an 'Un-alerted' ditching.

Ditching is NOT A TEAM SPORT! However, we need to be part of a team and clear the exit for the next person.

'1,2,3,4 out the door'

After our initial escape from an aircraft ditching, we immediately need to focus on the following:

1. Airway Management
2. Thermal Management
3. First Aid (stop bleeding and preventing Marine predators coming for a free dinner)
4. Group Management

Signaling

Again my disclaimer – this is purely my opinion on equipment based on my personal experience, please refer to your company procedures etc and if in doubt – ASK!

There is a multitude of signaling options available, so as before; we will look some of the common and simplest types available and more importantly those that can easily be transported through Customs and Immigration, however it is down to the individual to carefully select the equipment that works in their respective regions.

Many items (for example flares) are not permitted through Customs and Immigration without special permits and most flares can only be used once. Out of date flares need to be disposed of in accordance with local Governmental Authority Regulations, and for weight, durability and effectiveness there are far more effective devices available.

As discussed in the first part of Location, wherever you are, you will need to signal your location, even more so when floating in the water. Whatever you choose, remember most search aircraft look for color contrast – what ´doesn't look normal´ from the air for example. In my personal experience the ´International Survival Color ORANGE´ should be banned on land (and replaced with Blue as nothing in nature is blue), whereas at sea is obviously a better color!

The phrase ´needle in a haystack' REALLY applies when looking for persons in water. Think ´very small coconut in very big swimming pool´, if deceased, bodies look like black trash bags and are very difficult to see. FLIR is only effective if your body is still generating heat....

A whistle

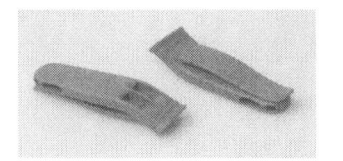

Sound travels very far on open water (why they have ´fog horns´ on ships and dangerous rocks). Choose a whistle without a ´pea´ inside.

Heliographs or Mirrors

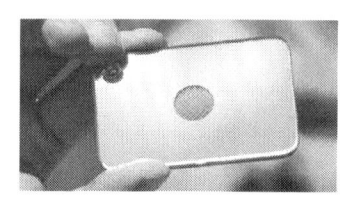

In the words of Tina Turner ´simply the best! ´. One of the best signaling items of all, and they can either be a purchased item or the inside of a survival tin lid kept highly polished. No moving parts, nothing that can break and visible for up to 24 km on a sunny day. They do require some practice in order to use them effectively.

Strobe lights

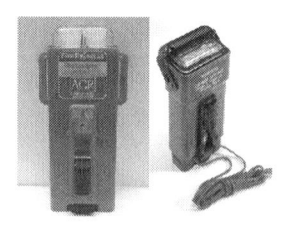

Highly effective at sea, especially at night, various options are available including the models that are automatically activated by water. If you keep your flight helmet on (Thermal protection?), then can be attached by simple Velcro patch to the visor cover / top of helmet, or the hood of survival suit, so it is always visible above water.

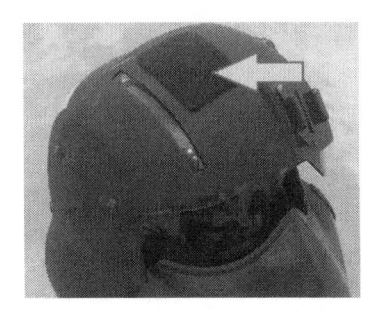

´See Streamer´

One of my newer additions of kit. Available on Amazon for approximately $80, and available in two models (20 or 40 feet long), this is designed to free float on the surface, and has reflective tape, plus cyalumes attached. It is the company policy to replace free of charge any that are used in a rescue!

Sea Marker Dye

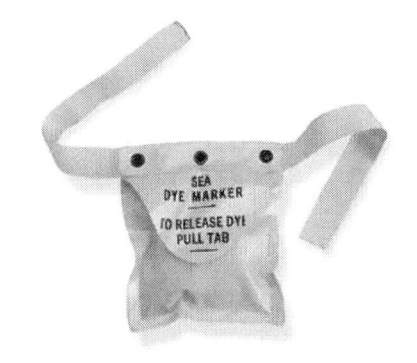

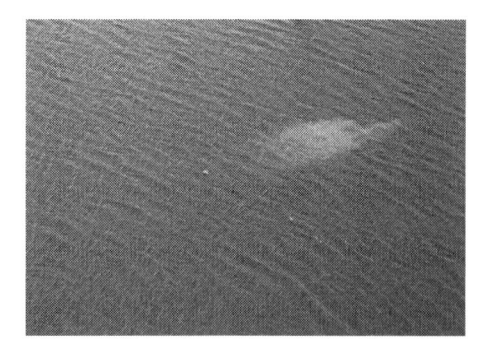

Not to be confused with shark repellent (which can be packaged very similar) and not really popular in current times, but extensively issued during the 1970s to Aircrew, it is essentially a bag of colored dye that you release into the water. With strong currents it dissipates quickly, so is a case (as with everything in survival) of using at the RIGHT TME.

Rescue Laser

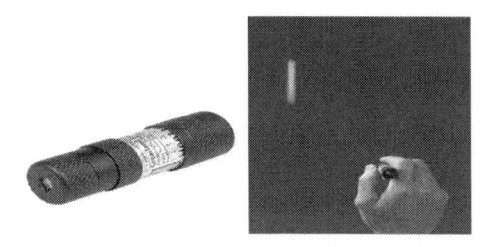

A relatively new device, the rescue laser when projected into the sky, gives an illumination area of approximately 6 miles that can attract the attention of passing aircraft. Unlike other lasers, this does not affect the eyesight of the Pilot and Crew. These lasers are specifically designed NOT to blind the aircrew, so unless you want you want your rescue helicopter crew sat next to you after crashing next to you..... Buy the correct and approved type!

Cyalume / Chemical Light Sticks

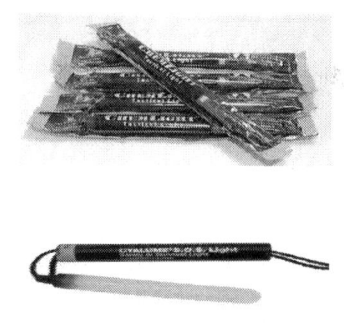

A very cheap and highly effective method of signaling at night, light-sticks can be used to mark individuals when walking at night, as illumination for shelters, marking paths and a multitude of other uses. With the addition of a length of cord and swung over the head in a rapid fashion they can be visible at night from approximately 2 miles (without NVG´s). These can be bought as a manufacturer purpose-built device or made you.

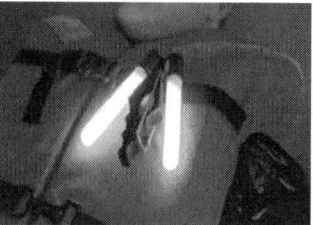

Personal Locator Beacons (PLB)

There are many different types of location devices available, from PLB´s (Personal Locator Beacons), modern PLB´s for example can transmit an emergency satellite signal that is accurate to 1.5 meters.

Surplus PLB/ SARBE beacons

These are available on eBay etc, and often look like a very cost attractive option. HOWEVER, they operate on the old 121.5 MHz satellite monitoring system (Not to be confused with the emergency distress channel). Approximately 6 years ago the US Government turned off satellite monitoring of this frequency. Modern PLB´s use the more effective 406 MHz – so simply, don't waste your money...

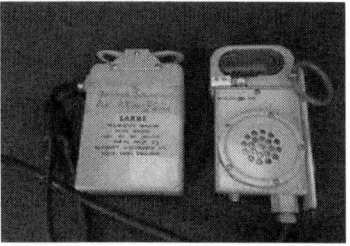

Pyrotechnics

There are two types essentially, the ´Rocket (or rocket/ parachute combination) ´or the ´Day/ Night´ flare. As I have mentioned before, not my personal favorite by any means, they can be effective if not used too early, but have major safety implications, many are very difficult to open when you lose fine motor skills due to hypothermia, and at night, if you get it wrong and drip molten magnesium on your survival gear/ liferaft – and are not rescued at that point, you may be in for a far worse day than you have already! A personal choice in my opinion....

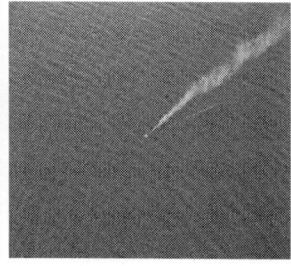

With minimal pool training, a group of persons in the water can create a ´carpet´, this provides both Thermal and Group Management, plus greatly increases your visibility!

Liferafts

You probably won´t have one of these! The FAA now requires a life raft on-board for flights over 50 miles overwater operations for Parts 121, 125 and 135 aircraft and for Part 91.501 over 100 miles overwater and come in many different styles. Difference between 50 miles at sea and being in the middle of Lake Superior for example? It's you in the water, not the rule book...

Yes expensive, but they

a) Get you out of the water,
b) Provide additional location and safety,

c) Contain extra survival aids and some even have their own emergency beacon (dependent on SOLAS category).

Offshore (Non- Coastal) Liferafts under SOLAS Regulations carry the following to assist you:

- Rescue quoits with minimum 30-metre lines
- Non-folding knife with a buoyant handle. If the life raft holds more than 13 persons, then a second knife
- For 12 persons or less, 1 bailer. For more than 13 persons, 2 bailers should be kept
- 2 sponges
- 2 buoyant paddles
- 3 tin openers
- 2 sea anchors
- 1 pair of scissors
- 1 first aid waterproof kit
- 1 whistle
- 1 waterproof torch for communicating Morse code with 1 spare set of batteries and bulb
- 1 signaling mirror/heliograph
- 1 radar reflector
- 1 life-saving signals waterproof card
- 1 fishing tackle
- Food ration totaling not less than 10000 kJ for each person
- Water ration- 1.5 liters of fresh water for each person
- One rust proof graduated drinking vessel
- Anti-seasickness medicine sufficient for at least 48 hours and one seasickness bag for each person

- Instructions on how to survive (Survival booklet)
- Instructions on immediate action
- 6 Hand Flares
- 4 Rocket Parachute Flares
- 2 Buoyant Smoke Signals

They can be rented if budget is an issue but faced with a 4-hour float in the water at night (which from personal experience is depressing to say the least), or a relatively comfortable wait for rescue……I know which I choose!

The procedure to follow once onboard liferafts are very simple:

CUT, STREAM, CLOSE and MAINTAIN

1. Cut the Painter (the rope line that may be attached to the aircraft to stop it floating away),
2. Stream the Sea Anchor to prevent drifting to far from your present position,
3. Close all the openings,
4. Maintain – Remove excess water, repair any leaks, maintain a lookout 24/7 with emergency signaling devices to hand, maintain body fluids: <u>EVERYONE IS TO TAKE 'SEASICKNESS' TABLETS</u> and maintain the principles of survival.

Water

If not in a liferaft then your ability to collect water is around zero. You might be able to take a drink from any emergency water that you are carrying, however if this becomes contaminated with saltwater, aircraft fuel spillages then will not be drinkable.

If in a liferaft then are options increase:

Rainwater

The easiest to collect and liferafts are usually designed to funnel rainwater to specific points where they can be collected

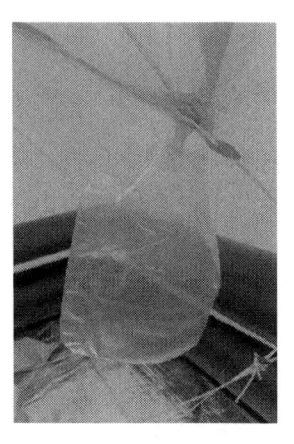

Solar stills

These inflatable devices are designed to allow the sea water in the center to evaporate and be collected after evaporation and running down to the outside of the ring, where it is drunk from a straw. Really efficient in flat/ calm water, slight waves can cause the sea water to mix with the fresh water.

Portable desalinators

Highly effective producing approximately 30 oz or 890ml of drinking water in 1 hour, their downside is that they are very expensive to purchase.

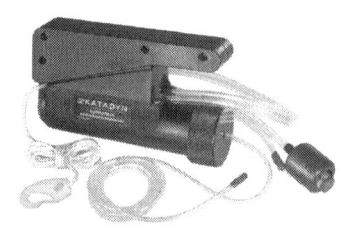

To put this into a real-world context;

On 17 November 2012, Jose Salvador Alvarenga from El Salvador set off on a professional fishing trip with his co-worker. A few hours into their voyage, a storm which lasted for 5 days blew them off course. They tried the radio to summon help, but then this and much of the rest of the boat's electronics began to fail.

A search party was sent, but after two days of looking and to no avail, the search ended and assumed they had drowned at sea. Alone and without food or supplies, the two fishermen survived off eating raw fish, turtles and rainwater. Weeks turned to months, and Alvarenga´s co-worker became severely unwell from eating months of raw food and died.

Alvarenga then endured another nine months alone at sea, until he eventually spotted a small island. Abandoning his boat and swimming to shore, he almost immediately met a local couple who alerted authorities. He had reached the Marshall Islands.

His journey lasted **438 days** and his voyage is estimated to have covered between 5,500 to 6,700 miles. He is the first person recorded in history to have survived in a small boat lost at sea for more than a year

Everything we carry is only a ´Aid to survival´, combined with an individual's ´Will to survive´...

PUTTING IT ALL TOGETHER

So, potentially a lot of personal equipment! Remember the key principle,

> *'We are dressing for the environment that we are flying OVER, not the nice warm environment (helicopter) we are sat in'.*

As our survival knowledge weighs nothing, we therefore need to organize our individual equipment sensibly, in a system that we understand.

As a rough guide to what to do with it all, here is an example of what we wear on a daily flight (a daily kit list), what we can carry as normal day to day items, a survival pack, and a '7-day bag' for times when we might be called to fly to another base that is not our own:

Daily Personal Equipment

- Helicopter Crewman Helmet
- ICS cords (extension, plus PTT extension)
- Aircrew survival vest with Life Preserver and HEEDS bottle
- Aircrew restraint 'wandering' harness (if individually issued)

- J knife for emergency egress
- Skull Cap (if worn)
- Long Sleeve Flight Suit
- Aircrew Immersion Suit
- Nomex undergarments
- Flight Jacket
- Flight Gloves
- Boots
- Torch
- Wallet with credit card,
- Phone

Day to day items

- Helmet bag
- Spare pens, pencils, notepad
- Phone charger
- Normal aircrew headset (in case helmet fails)
- Rain Gear
- Roll of tape
- <u>Small</u> individual first aid kit (band-aids, Prescription and personal medication)

Survival Pack

- Rucksack or 'Day sack'

- Firelighting kit
- Knife/ Machete (depending on terrain)
- Folding gardeners saw
- Sleeping bag
- Flysheet/ Poncho or Hammock
- Emergency Water
- Paracord

7 Day 'Deployment' bag:

- Spare Flight Suit
- Spare pair gloves
- Flashlight/extra set of batteries with ends taped
- Lip balm/Sunscreen
- 2-Water Bottles (filled)
- Sleeping Bag
- Socks (3 pair)
- Underwear (3 pair)
- Quick dry sports towel (1)
- Spare Prescription glasses
- Medications
- Uniform T-shirts (3)
- Set of casual pants (1)

- Tennis shorts or similar (1)
- Personal Hygiene kit/toiletries
- 1 pair of shower shoes
- Baby wipes / Deodorant
- Spare boot laces
- Small box of powder laundry detergent

These are just rough guidelines for what you could carry. We want to dress for egress, have any equipment to hand that we may need during a normal day, and then something to wear in case you get stuck overnight at a hotel (if it has a pool and you only have the flight gear standing in, you will be in a bad mood!

So how could we have a 'perfect world' take place?

Example:

You are working a 24 shift, one day on, one day standby/ training, and one day off. This process is repeated twice before having a week off (avoids fatigue, ensures a high state of unit readiness and training competence). You start your shift at 1000 hrs. (allows family time and no-ne likes getting up early!).

On arrival, you change into your flight gear as determined by the weather outside, and you meet your crew for that day. After requisite tea/ coffee you start the day at 0930hrs with a flight brief. The days weather forecast is briefed from available METAR by one of the Pilots, and any planned events (training serials/ PR flights etc), NOTAMS, any maintenance issues. As the brief only takes place for a maximum of 15 minutes, you are finished at 0945hrs.

On completion of the brief, the entire team, Pilots, crew, maintainers, EVERYONE 'walks the flight line' checking for Foreign Object Damage (FOD), anything that can be blown in the rotor wash, or sucked into the engine intake.

Once that is complete, and all trash disposed of correctly, your helmet, survival vest and associated equipment can be put into the aircraft. The Pilots do their walk round and sign for the aircraft, crewmembers do their own respective walk rounds and checks. The large 10-liter fire extinguisher and 'Start cart' are checked, and in position. The crew, flight line, helicopter is all ready to go and SAFE in an instant.

In monetary terms, what does that cost?

Absolutely zero,

Nothing at all.

Set up for success, and be part of the team, not a passenger.

Equipment / References

Equipment

Flight gear:

1. The original style flight suit: **http://www.sidcotflyingsuits.com**

2. Two-piece Rotor Wash flight suit: **https://www.stephanh.com/**

3. Touchscreen flight gloves:
   http://www.mypilotstore.com/mypilotstore/sep/13333

4. David Clark helmet conversion:
   http://www.davidclarkcompany.com/aviation/miscellaneous.php

5. Finger/ Lip lights: **https://www.flitelite.com/**

6. **https://priority1airrescue.net/shop/**

7. **https://capewellaerialsystems.com/**

8. **https://helicoptersonly.com/index.html**

9. Surplus flight gear: **https://www.flighthelmet.com/SFNT.html**

References:

1. Black Wolf Helicopters, Short Haul Operations, 2018

2. Black Wolf Helicopters ´Standard Operating Procedures´, heli-ops 01 to 15, 20187

3. Helicopteros de Guatemala, Manual of Operating Procedures, 2018

4. US DoT (FAA) Aeronautical Information Manual, 2017

5. US DoT (FAA) Circular 135-14B ´Helicopter Air Ambulance Operations´, 2015

6. NSARA Manual ´Helicopter Rescue Techniques´, 2013

7. FAA Brace positions:
   https://www.faa.gov/about/initiatives/cabin_safety/regs/acob/media/acob218.pdf

8. https://www.ncbi.nlm.nih.gov/pubmed/12688452#targetText=RESULTS%3A%20A%20review%20of%2084,%2C%20and%20pelvis%20(31.0%25).

9. https://aams.org/fashion-vs-function-just-how-necessary-is-fire-resistant-clothing-within-the-hems-industry-part-1/

10. Rice, E. and Greear, J. (1973). Underwater escape from helicopters. Paper presented at the SAFE meeting.

11. Glancy, J.J. and Desjardins, S.P. (1971). A survey of Naval Aircraft Crash Environments with Emphasis on Structural Response. Report No. 1500-71-43. Dynamic Science. Phoenix, Arizona: Office of Naval Research, Arlington Virginia. December

12. https://www.ncbi.nlm.nih.gov/pubmed/12688452 - Analysis of injuries among pilots killed in fatal helicopter accidents.

13. https://www.ncbi.nlm.nih.gov/pubmed/10135298 - The cost-effectiveness of air medical helicopter crash survival enhancements. An evaluation of the costs, benefits and effectiveness of injury prevention interventions.

14. http://www.faa.gov/pilots/training/airman_education/

15. https://www.faa.gov/pilots/safety/pilotsafetybrochures/media/oxygen_equipment.pdf

16. https://capewellaerialsystems.com/product/portable-helicopter-oxygen-delivery-system-phods/

17. https://www.amazon.com/Katadyn-8013418-Survivor-06-Desalinator/dp/B000F395X0

18. FAA Order 8900.1 Volume 4, Chapter 7, Section 4 accessible by visiting **http://www.faa.gov**.

19. (Flight Helmet Cords Can Impede Egress: Understand the hazard of direct-to-airframe cord connections): **https://www.youtube.com/watch?v=JMinY5tg5P0**

20. **https://www.omnimedicalsys.com/uploads/Tactical_Dehydration_An_Operational_Risk.pdf**

Made in the USA
Middletown, DE
18 August 2023